DETROIT: A STUDY IN URBAN DEVELOPMENT

DETROIT

A Study In Urban Development

by

SIDNEY GLAZER
Wayne State University

BOOKMAN ASSOCIATES, INC.
New York 3

PREFACE

I have presented a condensed narrative of Detroit's dramatic history. No effort has been made to minimize the contemporary pressures and tensions and critical urban problems. It is hoped, however, that the reader will readily detect a portrait of a beautiful, dynamic, exciting, and kind Detroit with a promising future.

I am indebted to many for suggestions and other assistance. One name, however, must be mentioned. Dr. Raymond C. Miller, my colleague, has given me much valuable information in many informal conversations.

CONTENTS

CHAPTER I

The Village Is Born (1701-1815)

The story of the origin of many cities often rests upon obscure and highly dubious accounts. This is not true of Detroit, however. It is clearly indebted for its location and establishment to Antoine de la Mothe Cadillac. He is the undisputed founding father. It was he alone who grasped the potential commercial and strategic significance of the Detroit River.

Detroit began to take physical form on July 24, 1701. On that date a flotilla of twenty-five canoes, comprising some fifty soldiers and approximately the same number of French artisans and other civilians, reached a site on the Detroit River south of the present-day Cobo Hall. This expedition, commanded by Cadillac, almost immediately began the task of building a fort and laying the basis for a community in the remote wilderness so very far in the interior of the vast—and only partially explored—French Empire in America. Yet for many years this outpost was to serve as a major gateway and cosmopolitan center for much of the Great Lakes region.

Few, if indeed any, were so well qualified as Cadillac to undertake the building of a settlement on the Detroit River. Cadillac had acquired his familiarity with the Great Lakes area before 1701. This capable but enigmatic French explorer was born in Gascony in 1658 of upper-class parentage. At the age of fifteen he left his native France for military service in the New World. Apparently, America had great appeal for him. In it he was free to test his courage. His marriage to Marie Therese Guyon, a Quebec girl, strengthened his American moorings. He repeatedly won the respect and confidence of his military superiors by the excellence of his varied performances in the service.

In 1694, he was assigned the command of the important western post of Michilimackinac. Here he remained for three years until his command was abolished as an economy measure. At Michilimackinac, he acquired considerable information about the entire Great Lakes area. He became thoroughly familiar with the many intricate operations comprising its Indian trade. He observed, at first hand, many of the mores of the natives whose friendship he desired. He also became aware of the growing English inroads and competition in the area.

We can readily understand his determination to challenge a decree that called for the abandonment of French administrative centers in the West. He believed that such abandonment would weaken the French defense of the important Great Lakes region and leave it an easy prey to conquest by the English and their Iroquois allies. Late in 1698, Cadillac set sail for the land of his birth. He carried his protests about French policy to many of his prominent countrymen. Finally he won the favor of Count Pontchartrain, Minister of the Colonies, and a major adviser to Louis XIV. The Count agreed that a fort should be built on the Detroit River with Cadillac as its commander. Cadillac was also granted the equivalent of semifeudal rights over a vast tract of land to be assigned to settlers. He returned to New France and completed his plans for a most unusual venture. He received little encouragement and the very minimum of official assistance from the administrators in New France. Nevertheless, with confidence and optimism, in June 1701, Cadillac set out from Lachine, near Montreal, to found a wilderness community.

Less than a year was required for the building of Fort Pontchartrain du Detroit—translated as Fort Pontchartrain on the Detroit (River)—and soon abbreviated to Detroit.

Cadillac's community began as a tiny village, adjacent to the river, between present-day Griswold Street and Wayne Street, and extending north to Jefferson Avenue. It was composed of a garrison, a mere handful of dwellings, and shops operated by bakers and other skilled artisans. Within this enclosure was also a church—St. Anne's.[1] Very soon Cadillac assigned long and narrow farms, which extended back from the river, to many of the settlers. These farms were later appropriately known as ribbon farms.

Originally, of course, the economic life of the community was primarily dependent upon the garrison. Cadillac, however, immediately took steps to convert Detroit into a major fur-trading center as a means of strengthening its economy. This was accomplished in part by inducing many Indian leaders of various tribes to locate their villages in the Detroit area. To the region came segments of the Huron, the Potawatomi, Ottawa, and even Fox Indians. Cadillac also secured modifications in the highly monopolistic fur trade to assure greater participation by Detroit residents.

In 1711 Cadillac reluctantly accepted a transfer to Louisiana, but he had firmly established the basis for a successful community. Detroit stands as a testimony to his intelligence, administrative talents, and skill in planning. Unfortunately, however, his arrogance, egotism, and envy prevented him from attaining the reputation to which he undoubtedly had aspired. Frequently his successors were officials with little imagination and, too often, they were devoid even of a feeling for the community. Luckily, however, they followed, in the main, the administrative pattern so successfully outlined by Cadillac.

In the very year of Cadillac's departure the Detroit area was the scene of a conflict. The Ottawas and Hurons at-

---

[1] Many Detroiters are not aware that the parish of St. Anne's is among the oldest in the entire Middle West.

tacked the Fox Indians, who had come from present-day
Wisconsin to establish new homes near Detroit. The French
commander, who believed that the Fox Indians would become receptive to English overtures, gave support to the
Ottawas and Hurons. Although the Foxes were crushed,
this action by the French was, in the long run, costly. For
many years the defeated Foxes and their Indian allies resisted France in Wisconsin and Illinois.

The Detroit community, however, lived in an atmosphere
of relative security. The almost impregnable garrison afforded protection from any potential enemy. Again the
habitants—the term applied to the permanent residents who
were landholders—could be thankful for Cadillac's vision
and care in planning the defenses.

Detroit was in every respect most cosmopolitan for a remote outpost. For the majority, life was gracious. All
accounts indicate that consumers goods were abundant. The
attire of the upper-class families clearly indicated an emphasis upon style. The dinners often resembled feasts and
gave evidence of leisurely existence. Families of means
entertained extensively and lavishly. Dancing began at eight
or nine o'clock in the evening and continued through the
early hours of the morning.

Education was, of necessity, informal. The priest, as
one of the few learned men in the community, assumed much
of the responsibility for elementary instruction. When the
population increased, a trained schoolteacher came to Detroit. His exact status, however, is a matter of conjecture.
Apparently wealthy families employed tutors, who gave
instruction in the academic subjects and in good deportment.

Administrative powers were vested in the commandant,
who combined civil and military authority. This official
listened to and made minor concessions, when necessary,
to Indians and *habitants*. By and large, the highly cen-
tralized and paternalistic French administration, with its

absence of self-government, met with a minimum of opposition. Only a few objected to a system that assured protection and promoted the lucrative fur trade.

Fortune continued to be kind to Detroit. By 1760 the community numbered over 2,000 inhabitants. The narrow ribbon farms extended some nine miles east to Lake St. Clair and an almost equal distance west to a point beyond the mouth of the River Rouge. Each year goods arrived by caravans from Montreal. These were sold to the *habitants* or exchanged for the valuable beaver and otter pelts of the Indians. The community was in frequent contact with the other major cities of New France. The personnel of the garrison, with its regular replacements from the mother country, afforded news of happenings in the Old World.

In 1760, in the course of the Seven Year War (1756-1763), known to the American colonists as the French and Indian War, Detroit was captured by an English expedition under the command of Robert Rogers, immortalized in Kenneth Roberts' novel *Northwest Passage*. Detroit's surrender to the British was necessitated by the defection of Pontiac, the great Ottawa chieftain. In 1763, the French accepted a treaty of peace whereby they ceded all except the remnants of a great empire to the victor. Thus, in 1763, Detroit officially became a part of the British Empire.

The influence of the French rule upon the future was not important in comparison with the length of time covered, neither was it as insignificant as many have implied. Obviously, self-rule as a policy was not fostered because of the governmental policy of retaining subjects in a state of dependence. Moreover, any community as far removed from major administrative centers as was Detroit was inevitably subject to a degree of indifferent supervision. The French had been chiefly concerned with the difficult task of successfully laying the foundations for a future metropolis. They had secured a degree of friendship with the Indians and accustomed them to the white man and his ways. Although their agricultural methods were regarded as crude as judged by later standards, sufficient food was produced to take care of the population. In fact, the stable and permanent character of isolated frontier Detroit represents the chief contribution of the French era.

The future pattern of the British policy was outlined as early as 1760. No effort was made to separate Detroit from Canada. The commercial ties with the French cities of the St. Lawrence remained. The upper-class *habitants* accepted British authority and worked in a friendly fashion with the new administration.

The Indians were less happy with the new regime. A general uprising in 1763 made the British keenly and painfully aware of a basic problem. The conspiracy had become part of the tradition of the entire Northwest, since it was organized and directed by Pontiac, the Ottawa chieftain, who hoped that a general uprising against all the major posts in the Northwest would free the area from a control regarded as oppressive. Although garrisons were destroyed by the Indians, the campaign against Detroit, guided personally by Pontiac, was a failure. Pontiac was ultimately forced to ask the British for terms of peace.

The new British rule did not lead to drastic internal changes for the Detroit community. The shrewd and very observant Jonathan Carver, one of the great New England travelers of the eighteenth century, said of Detroit:

> The river that runs from Lake St. Claire to Lake Erie (or rather the Straight, for thus it might be termed from its name) is called Detroit, which is in French, the Straight. It runs nearly south, has a gentle current, and depth of water sufficient for ships of considerable burthen. The town of Detroit is situated on the western banks of this river, about nine miles below Lake St. Claire.

Almost opposite, on the eastern shore, is the village of the ancient Hurons: a tribe of Indians which have been treated of by so many writers that adhering to the restrictions I have laid myself under of only describing places and people little known, or incidents that have passed unnoticed by others, I shall omit giving a description of them. A missionary of the order of Carthusian Friars, by permission of the bishop of Canada, resides among them.

The banks of the River Detroit, both above and below these towns, are covered with settlements that extend more than twenty miles; the country being exceedingly fruitful, and proper for the cultivation of wheat, Indian corn, oats, and peas. It has also many spots of fine pasturage; but as the inhabitants, who are chiefly French that submitted to the English government after the conquest of these parts by General Amherst, are more attentive to the Indian trade than to farming, it is but badly cultivated.

The town of Detroit contains upwards of one hundred houses. The streets are somewhat regular, and have a range of very convenient and handsome barracks, with a spacious parade at the south end. On the west side lies the King's garden belonging to the governor, which is very well laid out and kept in good order. The fortifications of the town consist of a strong stockade made of round piles, fixed firmly in the ground, and lined with palisades. These are defended by some small bastions, on which are mounted a few indifferent cannon of an inconsiderable size, just sufficient for its defense against the Indians, or an enemy not provided with artillery.

The garrison, in time of peace, consists of two hundred men commanded by a field officer, who acts as chief magistrate under the governor of Canada. Mr. Turnbull, captain of the 60th regiment, or Royal Americans, was commandant when I happened to be there. This gentleman was deservedly esteemed and respected, both by the inhabitants and traders, for the propriety of his conduct; and I am happy to have an opportunity of thus publickly making my acknowledgments to him, for the civilities I received from him during my stay.[2]

In 1763 the British by an edict known as The Proclamation of 1763 virtually barred American settlement beyond the Appalachians. Administrators apparently intended this prohibition to be temporary. They believed, however, that it was necessary for a time in order to avoid conflicting colonial land claims and to prevent future Indian antagonisms.

Detroit continued as a frontier trading settlement protected by a British garrison instead of a French garrison. The British relaxed the monopolistic license system imposed by the French. This new economic program intensified competition. The newcomers were men with British citizenship. Understandably, their activities were usually centered in the area adjacent to the fort. Within a short time the English section of Detroit assumed the character of a town. For the first time in Detroit's history, the garrison area became an entity somewhat distinct and separate from the rest of the community.

Eleven years of administrative policy, during which Detroit and the rest of the Northwest were often subject to a policy of governmental indifference and sometimes even neglect, were ended with the Quebec Act of 1774 which provided that the area should become a part of the Province of Quebec. The new arrangement seemed a logical procedure to British officials, who regarded the new program as a partial restoration of an administrative jurisdiction followed previously and successfully by France. It was not displeasing to the French population. The American colonies, of course, were angered by the measure which favored the French-speaking people.

---

[2] Jonathan Carver, *Travels Through the Interior Parts of North-America For More Than Three Years, Five Thousand Miles* (Philadelphia, Pennsylvania, 1784), pp. 71-72.

The outbreak of the American Revolution called attention to the importance of Detroit. The British realized that they must hold Detroit in order to retain control of the Great Lakes. They were also well aware that only the Detroit community had the economic potential to produce supplies for major offensive military action.

British activities were directed by Lieutenant-Governor Henry Hamilton, who aroused the enmity of Americans by sending out raiding parties against Kentucky and other remote and virtually defenseless western settlements. Indians who participated in the raids for Hamilton were paid only for the scalps they secured. This practice won for Hamilton the inglorious nickname "Hair Buyer." In 1779 Hamilton unsuccessfully took the offensive against George Rogers Clark and was forced to surrender at Vincennes. Detroit, however, continued to serve as a major British base. Additional military supplies were produced. The British continued to retain the all-important naval control.

By the terms of the treaty closing the Revolution, Detroit was included within the limits of the new United States. England, however, refused to withdraw from Detroit and other crucial Great Lakes posts. The English offered a pretext—the failure of the Americans to implement all of the terms of the treaty. Actually the English saw the great economic advantages from the fur trade.

Detroit gradually became the home of additional English merchants. Although this English commercial element comprised a small minority, it exercised considerable influence. It had wealth and prestige. Together with a handful of men of French ancestry, it assumed social and cultural leadership. Ironically, Detroit received its first taste of representative government during this interval of irregular English rule. In 1791 Canada was divided into Lower Canada and Upper Canada. For all practical purposes Michigan was made a part of the latter, which was granted civil government based upon English principles. This arrangement satisfied the Loyalist English-speaking population which comprised the majority of the inhabitants of Upper Canada. In 1792 Detroit held its first election to choose a representative to sit in the legislature of Upper Canada.

The United States protested, with regularity, the failure of England to abide by the treaty. For years, however, American diplomacy could not secure the desired concession. Finally, in 1794 when England was embroiled in a war with France, the American government made firm demands against England. In subsequent negotiations, England agreed to withdraw from the illegally occupied lake ports. These promises were made a part of the Jay Treaty. Accordingly, the British withdrew from Detroit in July 1796. For the first time the Detroit River became an international boundary.

Although the United States did not formally exercise jurisdiction over the Detroit community until 1796, it included the area in its early plans for western organization and growth. Fortunately for the future of Detroit, many accomplishments of the Americans between 1783 and 1796 were to aid in the development of the city. All of the present-day Michigan, of course, was made part of the Northwest Territory by the famous Northwest Ordinance of 1787. In a sense, this legislation served as the basis for the institutional development of the entire Old Northwest, comprising the present states of Ohio, Indiana, Illinois, Michigan, and Wisconsin. The Ordinance outlined a detailed plan of temporary government. In the same document Congress intelligently guaranteed basic civil liberties, prohibited slavery, and encouraged the beginnings of a school system.

By 1796 the United States had temporarily pacified the Indians of the Northwest. Many of the Indians had refused to acknowledge the jurisdiction of the American government. After several humiliating American military defeats,

President Washington directed General Anthony Wayne, better known as "Mad Anthony," to undertake a large-scale campaign against the Indians. His victory over the Indians at the Battle of Fallen Timbers (1794) and the subsequent treaty of Greenville (1795) removed the obstacle of Indian resistance to American rule.

The American soldiers sent to man the Detroit garrison in 1796 found themselves in a seemingly alien community. Here were some 2,500 people who had little familiarity with the United States. Their economic and political ties had been with Canada. The vast majority knew only the French language. The English minority who remained had, for the most part, British sentiments. A handful of the residents could claim German, Italian, or other European backgrounds. Included in the metropolitan area were several hundred Indians.

An immediate major task was that of Americanizing these people, making them conscious of the rights, privileges, and aspirations resulting from their new status. The introduction of new governmental procedures was, in itself, a problem.

The first county laid out was named Wayne in honor of the general who had defeated the Indians. In 1802 Detroit was incorporated as a town. It was largely through the experience gained by participation in town and county management that the early lessons of self-government were acquired.

Of importance also was the task of identifying the community with the new economy. These new processes were accomplished slowly but surely. The few Americans who moved to Detroit in order to engage in commerce comprised a real pioneering business element. The men frequently brought goods from Cincinnati; the Cincinnati newspapers brought the latest news. The contact with Cleveland and other recently developed Lake Erie ports was also important. This trade, however, never assumed large proportions. Fundamentally, Detroit was an isolated American frontier community. Often, in 1802, forty days were required for the transmission of a letter from Detroit to Washington, D. C.

In 1798, Father Gabriel Richard was assigned to the Detroit parish. This great French-born priest well understood the principles of the new American republic and successfully translated them to his parishioners. For over three decades Father Richard was to serve as a cultural as well as a spiritual leader in the Detroit community.

By 1805 the first transition to an American Detroit had been completed. The year 1805 is somewhat of a landmark in another respect, for it was in this year that Michigan territory was created, with Detroit as its capital. Previously the term Michigan, which was an Indian word for "lake country" was geographic and not political. Unfortunately in 1805, the village of Detroit was destroyed by fire.

It was fortunate for Detroit that it was the capital of a territory, since governmental officials were required to assist in its rebuilding. The recently appointed territorial officials reached Detroit almost immediately after the catastrophe. The new governor, William Hull, was a Massachusetts man with little imagination. Accompanying him was Augustus Woodward, one of the three territorial judges. Woodward was to sponsor various ambitious projects during his many years of residence in Detroit. He recommended that Detroit should be rebuilt according to a new plan which provided for wider streets. His proposal envisioned many streets to extend north from the Detroit River, in addition to the east-west thoroughfares. Apparently some of Woodward's suggestions were derived from L'Enfant's plan for Washington, D. C.

Woodward's project, of course, was carried out only in part. Many Detroit citizens were dismayed by the new physical changes. Gone were the physical characteristics of the town they had known. Months were spent by the governor and judges, acting as a land board, in making adjustments of older land titles. Nevertheless, a new physical Detroit gradually emerged. This new Detroit was American. The French language, however, remained the tongue of the majority.

Detroit served as a supply center for Michilimackinac, which was the headquarters for the American Fur Company dominated by John Jacob Astor. Although trade with Buffalo and other Lake Erie ports increased, the gains were not significant. In many respects Detroit continued to suffer from its partial economic isolation.

Always, however, there was a disturbing note about the future. This doubt arose from the fear of war with England. The English had built Fort Malden near the mouth of the Detroit River at the site of the present-day Amherstsburg, and opposite Bob-Lo Island, now the site of a beautiful amusement park. The fort was a threat to Detroit in the event of war. Another danger grew out of an Anglo-Indian alliance.

Governor Hull in his capacity as military commander had, however, taken steps to assure the defense of Detroit, so crucial for the control of the Great Lakes, in the event of war. When the struggle finally materialized as the War of 1812, Hull, on August 16, 1812, surrendered Detroit without even token opposition. To some his reasons seemed feeble, but he maintained that his action spared Detroit the ravages of an Indian massacre.

For over a year the Detroit community was subject to the administration of British military occupation. This second interval of British rule marked a low point in the fortunes of Detroit. All normal trade channels were disrupted. The residents were forced to remain within their community limits because they feared Indian attacks.

After Hull's surrender American military operations in the West, of course, centered around the recovery of Detroit. On January 22, 1813, an American force, comprised largely of Kentucky militiamen, was defeated at Frenchtown (present-day Monroe). In the aftermath of the battle an American remnant, including many wounded, was massacred by Indians in violation of a pledge of safety given by the British.

American strategists realized that control of Lake Erie was essential for the recovery of Detroit. On September 10, 1813, Captain Oliver Hazard Perry defeated a British naval force at Put-in-Bay. His famous victory in this Battle of Lake Erie soon forced the British to withdraw from Fort Malden. On September 29, 1813, American troops entered Detroit.

Although Detroit was regained by the Americans, much of the trading area remained under British control. Not until the Treaty of Ghent did Detroiters know a real security. Some of the trying days of this era are indicated in the following account:

> Three miles below Detroit are the Spring Wells, or Belle Fontaine. The bank is here about thirty feet high, and presents one of the finest views imaginable. You have a full view of the Canadian shore for ten or fifteen miles, Sandwich, Detroit, Les Cotes, and the wind-mills of both shores.
>
> The town of Detroit is situated on the western bank of the strait, nine miles below lake St. Clair and eighteen above Brownstown. . . . The town contains about two hundred houses, which are inhabited by more than one thousand two hundred souls; under one roof are often crowded several families. The town stands contiguous to the river, on the top of the bank, which are here about twenty feet high. There are several wooden wharves extending into the river upwards of one hundred feet, for the accommodation of the shipping; the largest was built by the United States, and is found very convenient for the unloading of vessels. The

principal streets run parallel with the river, and are inter-
sected by cross streets at right angles. They are wide, but
not being paved are extremely muddy in wet weather; but
for the accommodation of passengers, there are foot ways in
most of them, formed of square logs. Every house has a
garden attached to it; the buildings are mostly framed,
though there are several elegant stone and brick buildings.
Before the great fire in 1806, the town was surrounded by a
strong stockade, through which there were four gates; two
of them open to the wharves, the others to the land; this
defense was intended to repel the attacks of the Indians.

The fort stands on a rise of ground two hundred yards in
the rear of the town; the fortifications consist of a stockade
of cedar pickets, with bastions of earth; near the foot of the
ditch is a row of short sharp pickets, inclining outwards—
thirty pieces of cannon can be mounted on the ramparts;
the fort covers about an acre and a half of ground.

The proximity of one house to another, from lake St. Clair
to the river Rouge, gives the street the resemblance of the
suburbs of a great town. The farms are only twenty rods
wide on the river and extend back one mile and a quarter;
the same as those on the other rivers as well as those on the
British side. The country round Detroit is very much cleared.
The inhabitants have to draw their wood a mile and a half,
from the United States lands, in the rear of the town. It
sells in market for three dollars a cord; almost every farm
has an orchard; apples, pears and peaches do well—several
hundred barrels of cider are annually made, and sells as high
as six dollars a barrel. The land rises gradually from the
river to the distance of three hundred yards; it then recedes
till the country becomes low and level, and continues so
four or five miles, when it rises by degrees and at this distance is represented as first-rate land.

There are a number of stores which appear to have a brisk
trade, and they know how to extort an exorbitant price for
every thing sold.

The United States have a long elegant brick store at the water's edge, near the public wharf—this is completely filled with the spoils of the enemy taken on the Thames—and the arms of the volunteers. This building is eighty feet long, thirty wide and three stories high. The enemy had partly unroofed it, but it was soon repaired.

The streets of Detroit are generally crowded with Indians of various tribes, who collect here to sell their skins. You will hear them whooping and shouting in the streets the whole night. A few days after Proctor's defeat, the town was so full of famished savages, that the issue of rations to them did not keep pace with their hunger. I have seen the women and children searching about the ground for bones and rinds of pork, which had been thrown away by the soldiers; meat, in a high state of putrifaction, which had been thrown into the river, was carefully picked up and devoured; the feet, heads and entrails of the cattle slaughtered by the public butchers, were collected and sent off to the neighboring villages. I have counted twenty horses in a drove fancifully decorated with the offals of the slaughter-yard.

It is no more than an act of justice to the Indians, to state, that during their possession of the place, they conducted themselves better than could reasonably have been expected from savages. What they wanted to eat they took without ceremony, but rarely committed any other outrage.

The inhabitants are plentifully supplied with many kinds of excellent fish—the white bass, nearly as large as a shad, are caught with seins and in great quantities. The population is three-fourths of French extraction, and very few understand any other language. . . . They are excessively fond of music and dancing.[3]

---

[3] Samuel Brown, *Views on Lake Erie* (Troy, New York, 1814), pp. 92-96.

CHAPTER II
The City Emerges (1816-1865)

On March 29, 1815, British citizens from the Windsor area joined Detroiters in a gala "Pacification Ball" at Woodworth's Hotel and at its close former enemies parted with words of renewed friendship. Later, the Rush-Bagot Agreement of 1817, whereby the United States and England agreed not to maintain a navy on the Great Lakes frontier, strengthened this amity.

But only the most optimistic of the guests at the "Pacification Ball" could have foreseen any immediate bright future for Detroit. The War of 1812 had hopelessly disrupted its economy. Local capital for new business enterprises was seemingly lacking. Far worse, the hinterland could not be easily developed, since few prospective farmers would think seriously of venturing into southern Michigan—so frequently described in the East as a swampland.

In reality, however, the period of greatest handicap to future growth was over. The increase in population is but one index of Detroit's fantastic development. In 1820 the city, exclusive of outlying areas, had 1,400 inhabitants and ranked forty-seventh in population among the cities of the nation. In 1830 its population numbered 2,200. By 1840 its population had grown to 9,100. At mid-century Detroit ranked twenty-third, with a population of 21,000. Such significant gains continued. By 1860, with 45,600 inhabitants, Detroit had become the eighteenth largest American city.

Many factors contributed to this phenomenal growth. Very significant among them was the appointment in 1813 of Lewis Cass as territorial governor, an office he held for eighteen years. Cass dominated the political life in Michi-

gan for the three succeeding decades. He served ultimately
in the cabinets of President Andrew Jackson and of President James Buchanan. He was envoy to France and a
United States Senator from Michigan. In 1848 he was the
Democratic nominee for President.

Believing strongly that more settlers were needed in the
territory of Michigan to assure its future growth and development, the new governor began diligently to analyze
its various problems. To encourage farmers to migrate
there, he personally supervised expeditions to disprove the
prevailing notion about the non-productive farmland. He
immediately publicized his findings. He also took active
steps to guarantee local self-government and worked hard
to secure cessions of land from the Indians. In short, Lewis
Cass encouraged any program that would foster commerce
and promote the cultural life of Detroit.

Changes in transportation, however, were far more important to the growth of Detroit than the efforts of Governor
Cass. In 1818 the *Walk-in-the-Water*, the first steamboat on
the upper Great Lakes, made her maiden journey from
Buffalo. The arrival of the *Walk-in-the-Water* demonstrated
that steam vessels could successfully ply the Great Lakes.
It was almost a decade later, however, before steam vessels
became common, even on Lake Erie.

The major contribution to Detroit's great development
was the completion of the Erie Canal in 1825. This far-
sighted project, undertaken by the State of New York,
united Albany and Buffalo. In effect, it assured a relatively
inexpensive water transportation route between New York
City and the leading cities of the Great Lakes. Detroit immediately became a major beneficiary of a new commerce
and an increased migration.

Changes in transportation were not confined to the water-
ways. A network of highways, radiating out from Detroit,
was constructed in Michigan Territory. The most important

of these arteries was the Chicago Road which ran to Ypsilanti and thence through the southern tier of counties. This highway brought settlers to the famous Irish Hills area. The Gratiot Road linked Detroit and Port Huron. The Saginaw Road, uniting Detroit with Saginaw, paved the way for the settlement in Oakland County. The Territorial Road ran through the rich Washtenaw County lands and thence west. Stagecoach service added to the commercial importance of the highways. Prospective settlers moving to the interior of Michigan, or going beyond to settle on the Wisconsin shore of Lake Michigan, made Detroit their headquarters for shopping for supplies. Detroit became a major commercial center for many wholesale houses by serving this large and rich hinterland. The growth of the interior of Michigan helped to elevate Detroit to a new dominant role among the cities of the Great Lakes region.

Early Detroit, by its designation as the capital of Michigan Territory, gained tremendously. In this role it attracted many visitors on official business. Even greater significance was attached to the capital with the creation of a territorial legislature. This body held its first session in 1824. It was natural that Detroit was designated as the first capital of the State of Michigan. This distinction, however, was temporary. In 1850 the seat of government was moved to Lansing. The designation of Detroit as a federal land office and as a port of entry did much to enhance its commercial importance.

The development of the town in the years immediately following the War of 1812 gave some evidence of a new spirit and civic consciousness. In 1817, largely through the perseverance of Judge Woodward, the territorial officials established the University of Michigania, or Catholepistemiad, which was supported by public funds. Detroit's two clergymen, Father Richard and the Reverend John Monteith, comprised the first faculty. The latter was a Presbyterian minister who only recently had arrived in Detroit. He was the first permanently assigned Protestant clergyman in the city. Father Richard assumed six of the thirteen professorships of the university and the Reverend Monteith accepted the remaining seven. The university was never a true university in the true sense of the word, even after its more effective reorganization in 1821 as the University of Michigan. Nevertheless, it did serve to give advanced instruction beyond the elementary level.

In 1817 a newspaper was also established in Detroit. Father Richard had attempted to launch *The Michigan Essay* in 1809, but the time was not yet ripe for this type of newspaper. John P. Sheldon was more successful. His *Gazette,* founded in 1817, marks the real beginning of journalism in Detroit. Advertisements in the *Gazette* testified to· the increasing vitality of the commercial life of Detroit. The newspaper also gave its readers a summary of the "general intelligence," the then prevailing term for world news. In every respect, editor Sheldon contributed to the end of provincialism.

In 1837 the first city directory was published. Only a few facts about Detroit's some nine thousand inhabitants can be indicated here. The city claimed 1,310 dwellings and stores. Among the professional people were thirty-seven attorneys, twenty-two physicians, and two dentists. Four "first class" hotels were listed. The advertisement of a merchant tailor was only one of many evidences of wealth. Cultural life was evidenced by one bookstore. Five denominations testified to the spiritual life of the city. Several newspapers signified an aggressive journalism. The Michigan Garden, comprising four acres, was a recreational center. The owners expressed their pride in the growing menagerie and in every respect promised "a summer retreat from the hustle and cares of business." The number of theaters increased. The great ease in reaching Detroit from the East undoubtedly explains the presence of the outstanding talent which played before Detroit audiences. Improved transportation facilities also brought a very popular visiting circus each summer as an added attraction.

By 1837 Detroit was well established as an American city. Its economy was primarily dependent upon commerce, and the city became increasingly important as an administrative center. Detroit was not yet considered an industrial city, however, for much of the manufacturing was done in small shops operated by trained craftsmen, with but a few apprentices and helpers. Many of the products were sold to a local market by the proprietors of these shops.

Very gradually the market for products manufactured in Detroit was enlarged. The construction of railroads extending out from Detroit enabled its industrial leaders to reach a larger hinterland in the prosperous counties in the interior of Michigan. Foremost in contributing to the new commercial tempo was the Michigan Central, projected in 1837 as a part of the state-owned program of internal improvements. It was slowly extended westward through the second tier of counties. By 1846 it had reached Kalamazoo. It was then sold to a group of investors represented by James F. Joy of Detroit for approximately two million dollars. The new owners almost immediately extended the line to New Buffalo, on Lake Michigan. In 1852 service was extended between Detroit and Chicago. By 1854 Detroit also gained railroad connections with New York.

Another line, financed solely by private capital, added many counties to the Detroit hinterland. The Detroit and Pontiac Railroad Company, authorized in 1830, was completed to Birmingham in 1839. It was later reorganized as the Detroit and Milwaukee, and in 1858 it was extended to Grand Haven on Lake Michigan.

The pioneer railroad enterprises shared Detroit's rich rail revenues with other companies. By 1860 the railway network extending out from Detroit was highly significant. The East also gradually absorbed some of the products of Detroit that were transported by water. Of great importance, however, was the presence of men who could produce successfully in a competitive market.

Many of the earlier patterns of economic life contributed to the commercial vitality of Detroit. Significant among these was the Great Lakes trade. By 1850 exports from Detroit had become highly important: the major exports were flour, hides, lumber, beef, pork, and fish. Of basic importance, too, was the outfitting of immigrants who were on their way to new homes in rural Michigan.

The decade of the 1850's brought significant changes in the industrial pattern of Detroit. In 1852 a car works factory was founded to establish an industry that remained significantly important for half a century. Shipbuilding made great strides, and this decade also saw the growth of the tobacco industry.

Visitors to Detroit in the final weeks of the Civil War were impressed with the distinct commercial character of the city. Wholesale trade played an important role in the business life. Three dry-goods establishments, ten grocery houses, and eight pharmaceutical concerns sold only to the wholesale trade. Combined wholesale-retail establishments were not uncommon. Seven dry-goods concerns as well as fifteen grocers sold to the wholesale and retail trade.

Consumers could choose from a wide selection of retail shops for their necessities. The numerous dry-goods stores, groceries, and pharmacies were well distributed. The listing of thirty-six hardware stores was further evidence of the vital retail life of Detroit. Specialty stores included booksellers and tobacco shops.

Detroiters could select from fifteen restaurants, besides hotels, if they cared to dine away from home. Eleven billiard halls give evidence of the popularity of this leisure-

time activity. The presence of several hundred liquor establishments indicated that temperance education had failed in
Detroit.

The professions were well represented. Eighty-eight attorneys comprised the largest number of professional men.
The medical profession included sixty-nine physicians and
eleven dentists. The city also had three veterinary surgeons.

Commercial agents rendered many specialized services.
Eighteen Detroiters listed their occupation as insurance
agents. Activity in land sales enabled seventeen Detroiters
to classify themselves as real-estate agents. The cosmopolitan character of the city offered a livelihood to many artisans.
The building trades, of course, assured employment to
many. There were many listings of tailors, shoemakers, and
tanners.

An immense export trade was the base of this urban vitality. Large cargoes of unprocessed farm products—including apples, beans, cattle, corn, eggs, peas, potatoes, wheat,
and wood—were sent to the East. Bacon, beef, butter, flour,
pork, and vinegar were among the important processed agricultural products. Other manufactured products of importance included iron bars, pig iron, and lumber.

A pattern of city government slowly emerged. Although
a city government alert to the needs of its citizens had been
created as early as 1803, the governor and judges chose to
ignore its rights. In fact, the territorial officials were in no
mood to tolerate a strong city government. Accordingly, in
1806 the Detroit charter was revised. The mayor was virtually subject to the whims of the territorial officials who
appointed him. Detroiters, for practical purposes, were
without a responsible urban government until 1815, when
Governor Cass restored a degree of self-government. In
1824 Detroit was given its first real urban government with
a charter that provided for a mayor, recorder, and council
of five. The growing role of municipal government was

recognized in 1827 when the charter was amended to provide for the additional offices of town treasurer, town supervisor, and town assessor. Throughout these formative years of urban government the council was chosen at large. In 1839 each ward, which previously had been a convenient unit created to aid in fire fighting, was allowed to elect two alderman to the council. This geographic representation gave the Detroit city government a more popular character. The charter of 1857 finally recognized Detroit as a city. The mayor no longer sat with the council. He became a real executive with the power to veto the actions of the council. His powers of appointment were also enlarged.

The early limited character of urban government is well illustrated by the budgets. In 1830 the expenditures were $4,542. Included in this figure were appropriations of $356 for the Fire Department, $246 for public services, $31 for care of the poor, $63 for city printing, $68 for city courts, $1,153 for care of streets, and $445 for paving streets and street intersections. The salaries of city officials totaled $588. School appropriations were not included in the city budget at this time.

In 1840 the expenses of city government reached a total of $61,060. Ten years later the budget figure was $127,260. In 1860, the total was $294,436.

The 1860 budget included appropriations of $10,771 for the Fire Department, $40,667 for schools, $35,725 for public services, $18,912 for care of streets, and $33,309 for paving streets and street intersections. A total of $8,880 was appropriated for city lights. Only $186 was authorized for city parks. The care of the poor cost the taxpayers $11,625. The salaries of city officials totaled $18,947. Some $140 was set aside for the operation of the city courts. The interest on the city debt was $19,850.

Taxes were levied against an ever-increasing valuation base. In 1830 the total valuation was $711,680; in 1840 the figure was $4,610,951; and in 1860 the base was $16,213,832. This amount included a real-estate valuation of $14,027,133 and a personal property valuation of $586,690.

In the beginning of Detroit's corporate history the problems of government were elementary. Yet over the years the municipal government established a system of fire and police protection, provided good drinking water, founded a commendable school system, outlined essential public health policies, maintained streets and sewers, took steps to safeguard the public morals, and regulated markets to protect consumers. By 1865 Detroit had gradually endorsed a pattern of government which began to recognize the new urban character of the community. The mayor, no longer the recipient of an honorary position, was paid an annual salary of $1,200. Each of the ten wards elected two aldermen to the city council. The executive department included a controller, treasurer, attorney, marshal, receiver of taxes, director of poor, sealer of weights and measures, and inspector of weights and measures. The several commissions included a board of sewer commissioners, a board of grade commissioners, a board of health, and a board of commissioners of waterworks.

The municipal government also took more positive steps to assure law and order. In 1857, the Board of Aldermen created a special Recorder's Court in order to give a more judicial character to the court authorized in 1824. Three years later funds were appropriated for the construction of the Detroit House of Correction.

Undoubtedly, a dominant elite commercial class gave direction to the course of municipal affairs. Yet the rewards of municipal office were shared among the various occupations. John Williams, who was chosen mayor in 1824, was the first of several merchants to head the city government. Among the physicians to hold the office of mayor were Zina Pitcher and Douglass Houghton. The civic minded Doctor

Pitcher was one of the founders of the Historical Society of Michigan. He was influential, as a regent of the University of Michigan, in securing the establishment of the School of Medicine. Doctor Houghton, physician and dentist, won greater eminence as Michigan's state geologist. In 1841 he discovered the rich copper resources of the Upper Peninsula. Bankers and attorneys also served as mayors. Yet Andrew Meade (1834) was a seaman; John Patton (1855) a carriage maker; and William Duncan (1863) a brewer. Apparently, all economic classes shared in the management of urban affairs. The ward plan, despite its many evils, assured the presence of some cross-section of society on the Council. Although individual wards did not acquire the economic character of later decades, some areas could even then be designated as better neighborhoods.

A large number of Detroiters won political recognition at the state level. No one, of course, quite approached Lewis Cass, who attained national stature. Stevens Thomson Mason, however, most closely approximated a political idol of the people.

Mason, who was born in Virginia in 1811, was brought to Detroit by his father, John Mason, the territorial secretary. Upon John Mason's resignation from office, it was given to his son who was only nineteen years of age. The new secretary (later acting governor) almost immediately displayed qualities of administrative ability, a clear understanding of the basic problems of government, a real sympathy for the underprivileged, and an inherent capacity for leadership which were combined with a very pleasing personality. He also aggressively asserted Michigan's claims in the boundary dispute with Ohio which culminated in the semi-farcical Toledo War.

Mason shrewdly recognized the absence of effective partisan organizations. Two parties, the Whig and Democratic, had been recognized since the late territorial period. Politics, however, had remained largely personal in character and not closely related to national issues. The Democrats had led the struggle for statehood and had endorsed liberal suffrage provisions. In 1835 the Democrats, with Mason as their nominee for governor, won a sweeping victory. In a sense it was not at all strange that an individual twenty-four years of age, Virginian by birth, and a resident of Michigan by virtue of Federal appointment for but little more than five years, should become Michigan's first elected governor.

In 1837 Mason again led his party to victory. The Panic of 1837 and the failure to implement a state internal improvements program resulted in a reaction against the Democrats. In 1839 William Woodbridge of Detroit, the Whig nominee for governor, defeated his Democratic rival by some 1,200 votes.

William Woodbridge came to Detroit in 1815 as secretary of the territory. He later served as a judge of the Territorial Supreme Court. This Whig leader was conservative, highly intellectual, and slightly dour. He was the spokesman for the older families of New England background. He was sent to the United States Senate by the state legislature before the expiration of his term as governor.

Zachariah (Zach) Chandler also won recognition as a forceful political personality. He well illustrates the "new" type of leadership so often recruited from the mercantile ranks. His rise was phenomenal. In 1832 he opened a small dry-goods store. Soon thereafter he entered the wholesale trade and for several years he traveled through the area in which his sales were made. By the middle of the century he was among Detroit's wealthiest citizens. He served as mayor. Although he was a Whig for many years, Chandler helped to bring about the formation of the Republican Party in 1854. In 1857 he was elected to the Senate of the United States. Within the next decade he attained a position of national prominence.

Detroiters enjoyed spirited political campaigns. By 1839 political practices and techniques were well established. All parties made use of rallies and parades to arouse enthusiasm among their followers. A highly partisan press also helped to assure support.

In 1815 Detroit was predominantly French in character. Even in 1830 the families of French background were in the majority. During the next two decades, however, immigrants from New York, New England, and Europe poured westward by the Erie Canal and the Great Lakes, to swell Detroit's population.

At the mid-century Detroit had a truly cosmopolitan population. Of its 21,000 residents, 11,000 were born in the United States and 10,000 were foreign born. The largest number of the native-born citizens gave the state of New York as the place of birth. Natives of New England were also numerous. The Irish comprised the largest foreign-born element, but the German and English groups were also large.[4]

The thousands of newcomers to Detroit apparently adjusted rapidly to their new environment. Evidences of major economic discrimination against the immigrants are rare, but some anti-foreign sentiment was expressed at the meetings of the Know-Nothing Party in 1854. The extreme factions among the nativists, however, had very nominal followings.

The beginnings of ethnic neighborhoods, including the Irish on the near west side and the Germans on the east side, indicated that a modern city was taking form. Both German

---

[4] The country of birth of the major groups follows:

Germany	2,851
England and Wales	1,245
Ireland	3,289
Scotland	474
France	282

and Irish names were prominent on the roster of political slates. This was especially true of the Democratic ticket.

Changes in the educational and cultural patterns were as significant as those in the economic and political. By 1865 Detroit could with reason be proud of its educational progress. Yet as late as 1815 scant attention had been given to schools. At that time all schools were private. In some instances instruction was entirely satisfactory. Often, however, schools were operated by transient teachers with little background.

Fortunately, a pupil of this era recalled many of his experiences:

> The first school that I attended was in the spring of 1816, and was kept by a Mr. Goff and wife in a log house of two rooms, with fire-places and chimney between the rooms with a door connecting them, situated on the corner of Bates and Larned streets. Mr. Goff taught the boys in the corner room, it having two outside doors, and Mrs. Goff instructed the girls in their lessons, also in ladylike deportment and unaffected modesty, teachings I fear too often neglected under the present mode in our public school, her room having one outside door. The Goffs were Scotch. Mrs. Goff was a lady of kind heart, and a most estimable intelligent teacher, well liked by my sisters, who attended her school, while Mr. Goff, a short, thick set, red faced man, presided over the boys' room with ruler and rope. Every afternoon about recess time, he having by this time exhausted his half pint flask of whiskey, would detail one or two boys to go to a grocery and get it refilled, giving them a sixpence for the purpose, and woe to the boy that tarried by the way to test the quality of its contents. Every afternoon he would become so drunk as to require the support of his chair while standing up to apply the rope to the back of some boy or boys. The rope was knotted at each end. His habit was to double up the rope and throw it with almost unerring aim to the boy, who had to carry it back to the master, and receive a roping across his back and shoulders. The ruler was of black wal-

nut, and was used most unmercifully on the open hand, frequently upon both hands, of the boy punished.

The girls were sometimes sent into the boys' room to be punished by ruler or reprimand. In the school were many large French boys trying to learn English from the few books then in use.

The second school that I attended was started soon after the closing of Goff's, under charge of a Mr. Danforth, and was kept in a large one-story log house, fronting on Woodbridge street, east of Woodward avenue, in the summer or early fall of 1816. My father and mother had been very anxious for a school, and had assisted in obtaining scholars. Mr. Danforth boarded with us. The school-room had plain benches without backs, all around the room. In one end was a large open French fire-place, with chimney on outside. My seat was on a bench in front of the fire-place, the bench having no back, and my feet not touching the hearth or floor. There was quite a large attendance of scholars, both boys and girls. Mr. Danforth was a small, waspish, violent-tempered man, and I was nearly pounded and pinched to death by him. He would box my ears, frequently knocking me off the bench into the fire-place, merely for lounging, or leaning over to rest, as sitting on the high bench was a great torture to me, I being then not quite six years old. He would box my ears with both hands, alternating the blows after righting me up, by pinching my ears; frequently throwing a round ruler at scholars. He one day threw an open pen-knife at a scholar. That brutal treatment soon brought on earache, and nearly destroyed my hearing. My mother discovered that I was becoming deaf and stupid. This last defect I am aware was lasting, possibly was constitutional. She having one Sunday morning discovered my body nearly covered with black and blue bruises, ascertained the cause from my elder sisters, called in my father, and he brought in from the parlor Uncle Tom Palmer, and a Major Baker, who also boarded with us, to look at my condition. All were furious at the treatment I had received, and Major Baker swore that if Danforth were there he would run him through with his sword. It being Sunday morning and after breakfast, Danforth had gone for a walk, which gave sufficient time before his return for reason to resume her sway. He was then shown my condition, and appeared to be greatly surprised at it; acknowledged his hasty temper, and implored my parents' forgiveness. He was given an hour to leave the territory, and at once crossed the river into Canada. That was the last of Danforth's school—leaving me a life-long sufferer from earache and deafness.[5]

Undoubtedly Judge Woodward hoped to end this chaotic situation with his proposal for the University of Michigania in 1817. The jurist envisioned a plan of education at all levels, from the elementary through the university, under territorial direction. The failure of the University of Michigania and the reorganized University of Michigan (1821) to achieve collegiate status disappointed many. Until 1841, however, when the new University of Michigan opened its doors at Ann Arbor, Detroit had the semblance of university education.

The establishment of the university at Ann Arbor left a real void in the field of advanced education. This was remedied somewhat by the establishment of academies and female seminaries. The former were for boys and, in general, prepared their students for college. The female seminaries ordinarily offered a less advanced curriculum and stressed ladylike conduct and good deportment. One of the best known of the seminaries was the Detroit Female Seminary which attained prominence under the guidance of Mrs. Hestor Scott, during the years 1839 to 1842. All of these schools charged tuition.

---

[5] B. C. Williams, "My Recollections of the Early Schools of Detroit That I Attended From the Year 1816 to 1819," *Michigan Pioneer and Historical Society,* Vol. V, pp. 547-548.

In the meantime Detroit was gradually developing a satisfactory public school system at the elementary level. A territorial act of 1827 provided for a system of public primary schools. By 1832 Detroit had satisfactorily implemented this legislation. In 1838 all school districts in the city were merged into one district, a step which ended an educational discrimination that favored the wealthier districts. In 1842 education became free. In contrast, in many areas, even in the Middle West, the tuition in the public schools remained high for many years. In 1858 the Detroit Board of Education established a high school to serve students who ordinarily would have been unable to attend the private academies and seminaries. Parochial schools, conducted primarily by Roman Catholic orders, very effectively supplemented the public schools.

Civic-minded and influential men encouraged all aspects of cultural life. Of necessity the leadership was assumed by individuals with background and at least some leisure. Their joint efforts gave rise to an enrichment of life. The Detroit Young Men's Society, organized in 1832, set the pace for several groups interested in the advancement of culture. This society sponsored a number of lecture series. The learned men of Detroit spoke to its members. Its library, donated to the Detroit Public Library in 1882, is a further testimony of the interests of its members.

An interest in local history was evident at an early date. In 1828 a small group of prominent Detroiters organized the Historical Society of Michigan. Lewis Cass was the first president of the society, which sponsored lectures and collected materials.

Detroit authors were highly productive. Many of the early writers received their encouragement from Governor Cass. He used his official and personal influence to attract a group of younger men to Detroit and set them to work investigating the languages and folklore of the native Indian tribes. The most outstanding of Cass's proteges were Douglass Houghton and Henry R. Schoolcraft. Houghton was the author of a number of major geologic reports. Schoolcraft, who served for many years as Indian agent at Sault Ste. Marie and Mackinac, resided in Detroit in 1820 and from 1836 to 1840. He wrote extensively about Indian life and lore. The great New England poet, Henry Wadsworth Longfellow, drew his inspiration and data for his immortal poem *Hiawatha* from Schoolcraft's *Algic Researches*. Another Cass protege, Charles C. Trowbridge, was also a student of Indian lore. He was perhaps better known to his contemporaries for his research into the history of Detroit.

The novelist Caroline Kirkland was a resident of Detroit for nearly two years. Her experiences in the frontier communities of Michigan inspired the successful novels *A New Home, Forest Life,* and *Western Clearings.* The poems of the Reverend Divie Duffield were published under the title of *Poets and Poetry in the West.* The well-known teacher Lemuel Shattuck was the author of *History of the Town of Concord* (Massachusetts). History also claimed the interest of Henry A. Ford, whose *History of Putnam and Marshall Counties, Illinois,* represented very careful research.

Detroit's importance was recognized by many prominent visitors. Two Europeans who later wrote commentaries for their nations were among the distinguished visitors of the 1830's. On July 2, 1831 Alexis de Tocqueville arrived for a visit of three days. The great English journalist Harriet Martineau visited Detroit briefly in 1836.

American visitors of prominence were more numerous. Among the political personalities were Daniel Webster (1837), Horace Greeley (1848), and William Seward (1852). The great educator, Henry Barnard, spoke to a large audience in Detroit on December 5, 1842. James Fenimore Cooper spent some time in Detroit in 1848 to gather material for his *Oak Openings.* In 1845 Francis Parkman spent two weeks in the city to complete research for his *Conspiracy of Pontiac*. Another distinguished historian, George Bancroft, was in the city on October 6, 1849.

The public interest in and support for a library is further evidence of Detroit's cultural status. As early as 1817 a society was formed to establish a library. Ninety shares of stock, at five dollars each, were sold. The close relationship with the university is indicated by the decision to locate the library in the university building and to request teachers to serve as librarians. The library received assistance from the Detroit Young Men's Society and other organizations. In 1863 plans were made for a district library. In 1865, when it had some eight thousand volumes, the library was moved to the old Capitol Building. Up to that time it had offered only reference facilities, but with its removal steps were taken to convert it into a circulation library. In fact, the Detroit Public Library accepts 1865 as the year of its birth.

Book dealers assured Detroiters of the latest literary happenings. In 1817 John Sheldon, editor of the *Gazette*, established a bookstore. His shop was the forerunner of a number of establishments that promoted the book trade. This illustrious list included Friend Palmer, who took an active interest in Detroit's history.

The many newspapers gave Detroiters world, national, and state intelligence. The dailies were unusually well edited, and since the owners wrote their own editorials, they usually had a political slant. In fact, many of the dailies were almost fanatical in their partisanship. The *Detroit Free Press* is Detroit's oldest daily. It began publication on May 5, 1831 as *The Detroit Free Press and Michigan Intelligence*, a Democratic organ. Many specialized periodicals were published primarily for specific denominations or professions.

Little enthusiasm for art was developed in frontier Detroit. Yet, before the development of photography many of the prominent families were anxious to secure the services of the traveling portrait artist. Frequently these itinerant artists combined mural work and interior decorating with their portrait work.

Some of the portrait artists became Detroit residents. James C. Lewis, who came to Detroit in 1824, ultimately won national fame for his portraits of Father Richard and Lewis Cass and his sketches of Black Hawk and other Indian chieftains. The design of the first seal of Michigan is also credited to Lewis. J. M. Stanley did extensive work in landscapes and portraits. T. H. C. P. Burnham, understandably nicknamed "Alphabet Burnham," was a highly temperamental artist of Detroit during the 1830's. Although he did some portrait work, he is best remembered for his portrayal of crowds and street scenes. Robert S. Duncanson, an Ohio Negro whose training in art was financed by anti-slavery societies, had a Detroit studio during the 1840's. He returned to Detroit after the Civil War. Alvah Bradish, a brother-in-law of Dr. Douglass Houghton, was well known as a portrait artist. He also awakened Detroit's interest in art appreciation by his lectures.

The increase in wealth naturally brought with it a population able to purchase works of art. A successful art exhibition was held in Detroit as early as 1852. The development of the daguerreotype enabled many families to establish inexpensive collections.

Music, unlike art, enjoyed a receptive audience at an early date. There are references to pianos in the later years of the eighteenth century. Music has always been an adjunct of the church services. Secular music, however, also made an early appeal. A concert was given in Detroit as early as 1833 by an outside singer who was assisted by a local chorus. Brass-band concerts were instituted the following year and drew large and enthusiastic audiences. By the middle of the nineteenth century a large number of Detroiters played some kind of musical instrument. In 1847 the German community in Detroit organized the Harmonie Society, an amateur musical organization. The society soon claimed many business and professional people as members. The increase in wealth and in leisure made possible the formation of other amateur musical organizations throughout the decade of the 1850's.

Traveling groups of musicians became commonplace before the Civil War. In 1850 an Italian opera company from New York drew large audiences. In 1856 an English opera company also proved popular. Swiss bellringers and minstrels also became popular.

Many of Detroit's serious-minded leaders frowned upon stage entertainment. Others objected to the theater on religious grounds. This opposition, however, had diminished by 1850. In fact, by the mid-century, traveling companies and amateur groups won popular acceptance and played before enthusiastic, critical, and—sometimes—boisterous audiences.

The light side of life was much in evidence. Many of the activities were church functions, and some were under the auspices of the numerous fraternal organizations. The Volunteer Fire Department and other service organizations had their lighter moments, including the immortal "Firemen's Ball." Some organizations, such as the Detroit Boat Club organized in 1839, were begun simply to serve leisure-time activities. Skating and boating claimed the spare moments of many of the younger people.

Detroit's intense enthusiasm for baseball has pre-Civil War origins. In the spring of 1857 a small group of young professional men organized the Detroit Baseball Club. Undoubtedly, many other Detroiters envied the members who had sufficient leisure time to participate in the sport. Baseball also had a following among young men in a less favorable economic status than the members of the Detroit Baseball Club. These clerks and trade apprentices formed the rival Early Risers. The club was appropriately named since practice began at four in the morning and games were scheduled for five a.m. In 1859 the Detroit Baseball Club defeated the Early Risers by a score of 59 to 21 before a crowd whose sympathies were with the less fortunate Early Risers.

Detroit's religious history differs from that of many of the midwestern cities, since its early settlers were Roman Catholics. Detroit remained overwhelmingly Catholic until the great tide of immigration from New England and western New York in the 1830's. Although Protestantism was slow in establishing itself in Detroit, by 1865 all of the leading Protestant denominations were well represented. Moreover, two Jewish congregations, Temple Beth El and the Shaarey Zedek Jewish Society, were organized before 1865.

Many of Detroit's clergymen helped to shape the civic character of the city. During the formative years no member of the clergy could rival the stature of Father Gabriel Richard. In 1837 the Reverend George Duffield accepted a Presbyterian pulpit in Detroit. For approximately three decades he served as the "civic conscience" for the New England element.

Church membership, of course, crossed social and economic lines. Consequently, worship brought together individuals whose paths otherwise would not have crossed. The various denominations were awake to humanitarian impulses and sponsored the first relief agencies. In 1834 the Catholic Female Institution was created to aid the sick and the poor; in 1851 this became St. Vincent's Catholic Orphan Asylum. In 1845 St. Mary's Hospital, the first of Detroit's hospitals, was established by the Sisters of Charity. In 1836 the Ladies' Protestant Orphan Asylum was established by Protestant groups.

Some organizations were formed to assure greater security against the pitfalls of urban society. In 1851 the Working-men's Aid Society was formed as a mutual insurance organization to provide sickness and death benefits for German laborers. In 1853 the French-speaking population founded the Lafayette Benevolent and Mutual Society on a similar basis.

As Detroit grew, the burden upon public agencies became greater. An example of the problem concerned the care of orphans. A very severe cholera epidemic in the early 1840's greatly increased the number of orphans. Father Martin Kundig, the priest of the German Roman Catholic Church, was primarily responsible in bringing about a reform in the Wayne County welfare structure to assure more effective assistance to orphans and other county wards. The result was the establishment of the Wayne County Farm, sixteen miles out of Detroit. Contemporary residents know the location as Eloise. The Wayne County institution was far in advance of the typical and stereotype "poor house" of the era.

Detroiters gave their support to many reform movements. Beginning in the 1830's temperance lecturers spoke before large audiences. With few exceptions the speakers were sponsored by church groups. Among the more popular lecturers were the members of the Washingtonian Society, a group of ex-alcoholics who were able to win audiences with interesting personal accounts of their experiences. Washingtonians were perhaps not as persuasive as the Reverend John Gough, an unusually polished speaker with a national reputation, who spoke to enthusiastic Detroit audiences on the evils of alcohol.

Alcohol was not the only evil attacked by reform groups. Slavery forces also mustered considerable opposition. Support for the anti-slavery cause was more evident than in many cities of the North because, understandably, opposition was a traditional reaction in a state carved out of the Northwest Territory, where the Northwest Ordinance of 1787 prohibited slavery. Also humanitarian and democratic impulses strengthened the movement. Finally, considerable credit must be given to individuals who gave of their time and energies. Zachariah Chandler cast his lot with the anti-slavery forces at an early date.

A few of the Detroit anti-slavery zealots gave their services as agents of the Underground Railroad, a popular expression employed to describe the operation of a secret system of aiding fugitive slaves to reach free territory. The Underground had its agents, stations, and other auxiliaries patterned after railroad practices. Detroit was the northern terminus of the important Central Line, which operated from Cincinnati, across the Ohio River from Covington, Kentucky. Covington was a major base for slave dealers. Frequently fugitives made their future homes in Detroit, but some of them were transported to Canada in an effort to insure greater safety.

The contribution made to the Union cause by Detroit during the Civil War testifies to the vitality, patriotism, and generosity of the city. Union sentiment was high. After President Lincoln's proclamation of the opening hostilities with the Confederacy had been read from the wide steps of the Federal Building, measures were immediately taken to assure the proper military support. On April 24, 1861 the First Regiment of Infantry was organized. On May 2 it was mustered into service with Orlando B. Willcox as its colonel. On May 13 it left Detroit for Washington and claimed the distinction three days later of being the first regiment to reach our nation's capital. Other regiments in which Detroiters were numerous were rapidly activated. Regiment after regiment received its initial training and departed for the fighting area. The Second Regiment, with but ten days of training, left Detroit on June 5. By the close of the war, approximately six thousand Detroiters were in service.

Both the city and Wayne County offered bounties to volunteers. Financial assistance to men in service and allotments to their families called for large expenditures by the city government. Detroit also contributed a large portion of the total paid by Wayne County to the families of soldiers.

Various organizations also made contributions of money and materials to the various societies that rendered special services to the soldiers and sailors. The Michigan Soldiers' Relief Organization was formed to supplement the assistance given to the sick and wounded by the formal medical units. Various "drives" were held to raise money for this organization. Ladies' Aid Societies were formed to prepare necessary materials for the men at the front. Large contributions were also made to the Michigan Christian Commission which ministered to the spiritual needs of the men.

On one occasion hostilities were brought near to home, and Detroit residents received a real and sudden fright. Throughout the war Southern refugees and agents of the Confederacy had gathered on the Canadian side of the Detroit River. They had won over some Canadians to their cause. In September 1864 a small group of conspirators boarded the American steamboat *Philo Parsons* at Windsor. When the vessel was well out on Lake Erie the crew was seized and the *Philo Parsons* was taken over. Another small boat, the *Island Queen,* was also seized by the Confederates. A second force was expected to capture the annex steamer, *Michigan,* at Sandusky, Ohio. The leader of the plot assumed that the two groups of conspirators would be able to free the three thousand Confederate prisoners confined at Johnson's Island, near Sandusky, and use them as the nucleus of an armed raiding force against Union cities along the

Great Lakes. This would seriously cripple the war program at a most crucial time. However, the authorities at Johnson's Island had been warned of the plans and had taken the proper precautions. The conspiracy, of course, failed, and the *Philo Parsons* and *Island Queen* were abandoned by the Confederates.

CHAPTER III
Modern Detroit Emerges (1866-1900)

With the close of the Civil War, another new era began for Detroit. In 1870 it ranked seventeenth among American cities, with a population of 79,000. Ten years later there were 116,000 inhabitants; by 1900 the population had more than doubled itself. At the threshold of the twentieth century, as a result of a meteoric rise in population to 285,000, Detroit stood an impressive thirteenth.

The Detroit of 1865 was changing rapidly. Its economic character was transformed as new industries crowded out the small shops of the old. By 1880 Detroit had emerged as a major industrial city. It ranked nineteenth among the cities in the number of workers employed in manufacturing establishments. Its manufactured products were estimated at a total value of approximately fifteen million dollars.

Altogether the city was the home of some 825 establishments. The production of tobacco and cigars ranked first in terms of value of the product. The sixty-four tobacco establishments manufactured products with a total value of $2,716,000. Other major industries are given in the following table:

Products	Establishments	Value
Iron and steel	7	$2,498,000
Foundry and machine shop	27	2,466,000
Men's clothing	33	2,062,000
Flour and grist mill	28	1,992,000
Railway cars	2	1,795,000
Slaughtering and packing	7	1,721,000

The industrial development of Detroit was further accelerated after 1880. In 1889 industrial establishments gave employment to 38,000. The value of manufactured products rose sharply to $39,158,000. By 1899 shops and factories employed 54,000 workers, and the value of the manufactured products approximated $55,000,000.

In 1899 Detroit's industries were highly diversified. The seventy-four foundries and machine shops employed 15,900 workers. The 200 tobacco establishments employed 4,500. The furniture industry is not usually associated with Detroit's industrial history. Yet in 1899 over 1,400 persons were employed in twenty-two factories. The nine drug establishments had some 1,600 workers. Twenty-six establishments, with 1,300 employees, tended to elevate the production of men's clothing to the level of a major industry. Twenty carriage and wagon shops gave employment to 318 Detroiters.

Many favorable circumstances contributed to the fantastic industrial growth of the city after 1865. The first was the availability of adequate capital. Detroiters immediately took advantage of the National Banking Act of 1863. Even before the close of the Civil War two national banks were in operation. This adequacy of capital helped to supply funds for economic expansion. In 1882 Detroit had twelve banks with a combined capital stock of some $3,610,000 and deposits of approximately $17,000,000. In 1900, the twenty-seven banks in the city had assets of $82,000,000. Some industrialists, of course, did not resort to borrowing. These men expanded their establishments from their profits.

Detroit was never a major railway center. Yet by 1890 it had all the benefits of the national railroad system. In addition, the completion of a network of railroads in Michigan drastically enlarged the Detroit hinterland.

Detroit's prominence as a wholesale center also aided manufacturing. Many of the wholesalers purchased from local manufacturers. These wholesalers employed traveling salesmen as representatives. Hundreds of retailers visited

Detroit several times throughout the year in order to make their large seasonal purchases. A few wholesalers even manufactured a larger portion of their products in the city.

A number of Detroit specialty manufacturers sold their products to a national or international market. This·was true in particular of the manufacturers of drugs, tobacco, and paint. Other Detroit industrialists, who sold primarily to the local market, were among the first to recognize the importance of new consumer patterns. Finally, Detroit's industrial growth was stimulated by many enterprising men.

Representative examples will indicate the stature of Detroit industries. The Michigan Stove Company, which began production in 1872, employed 1,000 workers within a decade after its establishment. Its Garland stoves were sold nationally. The company had several regional branches, including one in Sacramento, California. Detroit tobacco companies introduced many "brand names" that were popular in every region of the nation. Parke, Davis, and Company and the Frederick Stearns Pharmaceutical Manufacturing Company sold their drugs throughout the nation.

Many thousands of people, of course, migrated to Detroit because of its unusual economic opportunities. Although the native-born residents came from all parts of the United States, the migration from rural Michigan was large. The foreign-born continued to constitute a large and significant element in Detroit's population, and by 1880 comprised 45,000 of the 116,000 residents. The Germans were the most numerous. The Canadians, English, Scotch, and Irish also constituted important elements of the population. Other nationalities were represented in small numbers.

In 1900 approximately 96,000 of Detroit's 285,000 residents were of foreign birth. The 32,000 Germans comprised the largest foreign-born group. Many Canadians were attracted to Detroit after 1880. In 1900 the city was the home of 25,400 English-speaking and 3,500 French-speaking Canadians. The English numbered 6,300; the Scotch 2,500; and the Irish 6,400. The 14,000 Polish immigrants also comprised a significant element in Detroit's population.[6]

Many of the ethnic groups undertook an institutional development to preserve their ways or to engage in philanthropic endeavors. Often the organizations were small and little known, except by their members. All of these organizations, however, ultimately aided the immigrant to live a new life in Detroit.

Detroiters lived in clearly identifiable neighborhoods. Some neighborhoods were ethnic; others were economic; a few were ethnic-economic. The most picturesque and publicized, of course, were the nationality neighborhoods. Many of the Irish lived in the lower West Side. Although numerous Germans were found in various areas throughout the city, the most distinct neighborhoods were located around Gratiot Avenue. A definite Jewish neighborhood had its center at Gratiot and Hastings, at the point where the Walter Chrysler Expressway intersects Gratiot.

Each of the nationality neighborhoods rendered distinct services. In non-English speaking sections, the use of the native language was, of course, important. In all of the ethnic neighborhoods, however, were to be found professional men and the wealthier business people who could command the confidence of men and women of a similar na-

---

[6] Other nationality groups included:

Austrians	471
Belgians	671
Bohemians	612
Danes	231
French	589
Dutch	397
Italians	905
Russians	1,332
Swedes	267
Swiss	491

tionality background. The business establishments were also very significant as economic and social centers.

Detroit, however, had fewer tight and compartmentalized ethnic sections than did many cities of a similar size. Many nationalities that ordinarily lived in compact groups were not found in large numbers in Detroit. The high rate of social mobility also seemed to lead to disintegration, and families of means often left the old neighborhood. Assimilation, likewise, seems to have been rapid, for the majority apparently wanted to become a part of the dominant culture.

As a result, the more common basis for the neighborhood was economic-social. The limits of all such groupings were loosely defined. Not infrequently the neighborhood possessed an informal name, like that of a nearby school. These neighborhoods, which helped to determine the character of the city, rendered many of the services of the highly publicized frontier rural community. Credit was essential for lower-income families and was made possible by the "corner" grocer and butcher. The physician also extended credit.

Neighbors frequently gave assistance in the event of illness. They offered sympathy and on special occasions, such as weddings and receptions, loaned furniture. Young people were, of course, often annoyed when the older generation, with the best of intentions, passed judgment upon the youth of the community. Higher-income groups were less dependent upon neighbors for assistance. Transient areas also possessed fewer characteristics of "togetherness."

Visitors in Detroit were ordinarily favorably impressed. Willard Glazier, in his *Peculiarities of American Cities,* gives an almost flattering description:

> Detroit, the fair "City of the Strait," spreads itself along the river front for miles, and the approach from Windsor, on the opposite shore, is suggestive of the pictured lagoons of

Venice, Queen of the Adriatic. The Detroit River, or strait, is one of the most beautiful water avenues west of the Hudson. It is from half a mile to a mile wide, is always of a clear green color, and is never troubled by sand bars or anything which might affect its navigation. It has an average depth of twenty-five feet at the wharves and perhaps forty or fifty feet in the centre of the river bed. No floods disturb its calm flow or change the pervading green of its waters. It is, with reason, the pride of the city, and the ferry boats of the several lines plying between Detroit and Windsor are of the most attractive type. In summer a corps of musicians are [sic] engaged for the regular trips, and are [sic] considered as indispensable to the boat's outfit as the captain or pilot. Their syren strains entice the lounger at the wharf, and he may ride all day, if he chooses, for the sum of ten cents. Whole families spend the day on the river, in this way, taking their dinner in baskets, as they would go to a picnic. The people of Detroit, perhaps, inherit the pleasure-loving characteristics of their French ancestors, or at least they do not seem to have their minds exclusively concentrated on the struggle after the almighty dollar. . . .

Among the first objects of interest which attract the stranger's attention are the new City Hall and the Soldiers' Monument. The City Hall, fronting on one side of the square known as the Campus Martius, is a structure of which any city in the land might be proud. It is built of Cleveland sandstone, and faces on four streets—being two hundred feet long on Woodward avenue and Griswold street, with a width of ninety feet on Fort street and Michigan avenue.

It is built in the style of the Italian renaissance, with Mansard roof and a tower rising from the centre of the building, adorned at its four corners with colossal figures fourteen feet high, representing "Justice," "Industry," "Arts," and "Commerce." Its height from the ground to the top of the tower is a hundred and eighty feet, and the three ample stories above the basement furnish accommodation to the city and county offices, in addition to the Circuit and Recorder's

Courts. The walls are frescoed, the floors laid in mosaics of colored marbles, and the Council Chamber and other public rooms are furnished with black walnut chairs and desks, and paneled in oak. With these exceptions, there is no woodwork about the immense building. Everything, from basement to dome, is brick and iron and stone. Even the floors are built in delicate arches of brick and iron, and iron staircases follow the windings of the tower to its dizzy top. It is reckoned fireproof. The exterior is curiously carved, and two large fountains adorn the inclosing grounds. The estimated cost of the building is about six hundred thousand dollars.

From the airy outlook of the City Hall Tower, Detroit appears like a vast wheel, many of whose streets diverge like spokes from this common centre, reaching outward until they touch, or seem to touch, the wooded rim of the distant horizon. The hub of this wheel is the triangular public square called the Campus Martius, and the Soldiers' Monument is also the centre of this imaginary hub. Michigan avenue—one of the long arms of the wheel—loses itself in the western distance, and is called the Chicago road. Woodward avenue leads into the interior, toward Pontiac, and Gratiot avenue goes in the direction of Port Huron. Fort street, in yet another direction, guides the eye to Fort Wayne and the steeples of Sandwich, four miles away. Toward the southern or river side of the city, the resemblance to the wheel is nearly lost, and one sees nothing but compact squares of blocks, cut by streets crossing each other at right angles and running parallel and perpendicular to the river. Between the Campus Martius and Grand Circus Park there are half a dozen or more short streets, which form a group by themselves, and break in somewhat on the symmetry of the larger wheel, without destroying it. This point gives the best view of Detroit to be obtained anywhere about the city.

The Soldiers' Monument is a handsome granite structure, fifty-five feet in height, the material of which was quarried from the granite beds of Westerly, Rhode Island, and modeled into shape under the superintending genius of Randolph Rogers, of Rome, Italy. It is surmounted by a massive allegorical statue, in bronze, of Michigan, and figures of the soldier and sailor, in the same material, adorn the four projections of the monument; while bronze eagles with spread wings are perched on smaller pedestals in the intermediate spaces. Large medallions, also in bronze, with the busts of Grant, Lincoln, Sherman and Farragut, in low relief, cover the four sides of the main shaft, and higher up the following inscription is imprinted against the white background of granite:—

"Erected By The People Of Michigan
In Honor Of The Martyrs Who Fell
And The Heroes Who Fought
In Defence Of Liberty And Union."

The bronzes and ornaments were imported from the celebrated foundry at Munich, Bavaria, and the cost of the monument—donated exclusively by private subscription—amounted to fifty-eight thousand dollars. The unveiling of the statute took place April ninth, 1872.

Another feature of the city is the Public Library, founded in March, 1865, and at present occupying the old Capitol, until the new and elegant Library building now in process of construction is completed.

Beginning entirely without funds, ten years ago, it can now exhibit a muster roll of twenty-five thousand volumes, and is fairly started on the high road to fortune. There is a kind of poetic justice in the fact that its principal source of revenue accrues from county fines and penalties. Here is a knotty question for the divinity doctors, for in this case, at least, good is born of evil. The library is under the control of the Board of Education, and was given an existence from the State constitution. Some very rare volumes of Mexican antiquities have recently been purchased from England by the School Board and added to the library, at a cost of four hundred dollars. They contain a pictorial and hieroglyphic history of the Aztec races occupying Mexico when Cortes came over from a foreign shore with his Spanish galleons.

The earliest date goes back to 1324, and the strange figures in the centre of the page are surrounded by devices indicating cycles of thirteen years, four of which made a great cycle, or a period of fifty-two years. The deeds of the Aztec king, *Tenuch,* and his successors, are here recorded, and through the efforts of an English nobleman who devoted his life to these researches, we have the translation rendered for us.

The city has a scientific association, two years old, and also a Historical Society, in which her citizens manifest considerable pride.

Detroit has been called, with reason, one of the most beautiful cities of the West. Transformed from the ancient *Teushagrondie* into the present populous "City of the Strait," she sits like a happy princess, serene, on the banks of her broad river, guarding the gates of St. Clair.[7]

Many men of stature assumed political leadership and in a sense, civic leadership. All were individuals of some means, with deep roots and moorings. James McMillan came up from the ranks. He invested in a large number of companies in Detroit and in other Michigan cities. During the 1890's he dominated the Republican Party on a city and state level. He was, in fact, one of the few men in Michigan, with the exception of Chandler, to exercise his power in the politics of the state. His influence made possible his election to the Senate of the United States.

Thomas Palmer was less forceful than McMillan. His counsel, however, was sought by all influential groups in Detroit. Palmer's name was associated with many philanthropies. Although he served in the Senate of the United States, his influence in the Republican Party on the state level was nominal.

---

[7] Willard Glazier, *Peculiarities of American Cities,* Philadelphia, Pennsylvania. 1884, pp. 184-193.

In 1884, General Russell A. Alger, the Republican nominee for governor, defeated his Democratic rival in a hotly contested contest. This victory elevated Alger to a position of prominence with the party. Alger's record in the Civil War had been most unusual. He had volunteered as a private in the Second Michigan Cavalry and had risen, by 1865, to the rank of major general. At the close of the Civil War he settled in Detroit and acquired a fortune in the thriving lumber industry. In 1888 he mustered considerable strength for the Republican nomination for the presidency. Alger was Secretary of War during the Spanish-American War. Alger gave assistance to many Detroit civic and philanthropic ventures.

Donald Dickinson was an outstanding Detroit and Michigan Democrat who belonged to the conservative wing of the party. He was regarded as among the outstanding legal minds in the Middle West. He served briefly as Postmaster-General in the first Cleveland administration.

The most popular of the political leaders, however, was Hagen Pingree, a highly successful shoe manufacturer who entered politics when he was middle-aged. In 1889 he was successfully nominated and elected mayor by the Detroit Republicans, even though the Democratic Party at the time exercised real power in city politics. Because slipshod methods of urban management could no longer be tolerated, Pingree set out to apply business methods. Although he soon discovered that old-time urban political leaders were thwarting him, he stood his ground and won with popular support, not, however, without making enemies of many old-time political leaders. He won further public support when he secured lower streetcar fares. He gradually acquired the label of "reformer."

Pingree's stature in Michigan and even beyond its limits was the result of his attempts to help the Detroit needy during the Panic of 1893. When the number of unemployed in the city became alarmingly large, Mayor Pingree proposed to alleviate their plight by assigning small plots of vacant land to them. This plan enabled many to raise some of their food. Press reaction to this was favorable throughout the nation. Pingree was hailed as a mayor who was at least aware of the problem and was trying to solve it.

In 1896 Pingree's stature was such that he was nominated and elected governor by the Republicans, serving for one year as both governor and mayor. In 1898 he was re-elected. His record as governor proved him to be a true reformer.

Pingree has often been hailed as a progressive. Undoubtedly, he subscribed to many of the principles and goals of this school of thought. Beyond a doubt he won the reputation of a reform mayor. This was, in part, due to his determination to guarantee low public transportation fares to the citizens of Detroit. This public transportation issue dated back to 1863 and was not easily solved. At that time the city authorized the Detroit City Railways to operate horse-drawn cars at a speed not to exceed six miles per hour and only to operate on designated major streets. The plans of the company, however, did not provide for service on Fort Street, and in 1864 the Fort Street Railway was given a charter. The limited capital of the companies meant that many areas were without service. This, in turn, resulted in the formation of additional splinter companies.

By the late eighties conditions were chaotic. New equipment and improved service were required by Detroiters. Large-scale capital could only be secured by the consolidation of lines and the procurement of long-term loans. The latter could be secured only if investors were assured of lengthy and favorable franchises.

The city government, under Pingree in particular, demanded more restrictive franchises and pledges of lower fares and better service. Each side won concessions. By 1900 the Detroit lines were consolidated into the Detroit

United Railway (D.U.R). This electrified system, comprising over two hundred miles of routing, was financially strong and capable of rendering services to a growing metropolis. As it was a monopoly, its future became a major political issue.

Pingree's appeal to the electorate, at least in part, was the awareness that he could offer a bold, honest, and progressive leadership. Detroiters well understood that the problems of city government were becoming highly complex. They knew that a reform government must of necessity have the mayor as its champion.

Although Detroiters desired an efficient use of their tax dollars, they did not oppose an enlargement of municipal services. In 1860 the city budget called for expenditures of $294,000. Ten years later the figure was $693,000. In 1881 the City Council gave its approval to a budget of $902,000. Of this amount $183,000 was appropriated for schools. The Police Department received $135,000 and the Fire Department $111,000. Appropriations for street paving and the "care of streets" were approximately $91,000. The city fathers authorized $24,000 for the care of the poor.

The Democrats and Republicans were almost evenly matched in the bitterly fought partisan elections. The successful candidate for mayor often won only by the narrowest of margins. Each party was well represented on the powerful City Council. In municipal elections many Detroit voters were "independents" who ignored the pleas for party regularity. Although the Democrats remained a powerful force in municipal politics, the party gradually lost ground in the elections for national, state, and county offices. The Republicans were strengthened by an effective leadership. On the other hand, the Democrats suffered from major internal dissensions.

The "power structure" was frequently modified. The men who held office came from cross-sections of the population. After 1889, in particular, "balanced" Democratic and Republican slates included many from recognized ethnic and labor groups.

In general, the extension of basic governmental services progressed rapidly. In 1900 the Police Board supervised a well-trained department with personnel numbering five hundred. Six neighborhood precinct stations supplemented the services of the central or headquarters station. The highly modernized Fire Department personnel numbered 476. Detroit residents were assured an adequate and "safe" water supply. The water from the Detroit River was purified at a station four and one-half miles east of Woodward. The Water Department boasted that it was able to supply even the most recently developed portions of the city with water.

Between 1880 and 1900 the municipal government provided Detroit residents with adequate parks. The enlargement of the park system, in part, grew out of a popular demand for a more sophisticated recreational environment. Undoubtedly the city fathers found it difficult to deny the requests of park partisans who pointed to the example of Central Park in New York.

The capstone of the new park plan was Belle Isle. This island of approximately seven hundred acres in the Detroit River extended from Lake St. Clair to within three miles of Woodward Avenue. Early in the nineteenth century it contained neglected farms and was known as Hog Island because of the numerous wild hogs. After 1865 it became an informal picnic ground for many Detroiters. In 1879 the owners of Belle Isle sold this choice property to the city for $180,000. However, no immediate plans for improvement were made. Many argued that the property should be sold. In 1881 the City Council rejected an offer of $225,000 for Belle Isle and recommended the establishment of a park with adequate recreational facilities.

itigate pauperism was accepted by the city gov-
ithout opposition.

the Poor Commission gave assistance to 189 mar-
es, 175 widows, fifty-four deserted wives, eight
se husbands were in prison, one wife whose hus-
in an institution for the insane, ten widowers and
people. The Commission reported that 176 were
stance because of sickness, twenty-eight because
oyment, thirty-two because of old age, and three
f too-large families.

County naturally bore the brunt of the long-term
lem. The budget for the county institutions was
Gains were made in the treatment of mental

depression years between 1893 and 1896 the wel-
lem was, of course, acute. However, the great
of Detroit laborers did not find it necessary, under
onditions, to ask for assistance. Undoubtedly they
er conditions more satisfactory than those in many

n must be exercised in discussing standards of liv-
asurements for the kinds of comforts enjoyed during
nineteenth century differ considerably from our
e standard of living was affected by several factors
prices, and unemployment. All evidence, however,
dicate that as a result of the increase of real income,
s of living became demonstrably higher. In the long
he period between 1865 and 1900, the standard of
creased for all economic classes in Detroit through
dening of the base of social services. The exten-
educational facilities gave a general opportunity
d economic and social mobility. In some instances,
r, the wage paid to the unskilled was sufficient only
the very minimum of human requirements.

The Commission of Parks and Boulevards took steps to convert Belle Isle Park into another Central Park. The Commission secured the services of the great landscape artist Frederick Law Olmstead, creator of Central Park. He planned a system of driveways, canals, and artificial lakes to give Belle Isle the character of a resort.

Each year thousands of Detroiters and visitors enjoyed the Belle Isle "outing." Transportation to the park was relatively inexpensive for the many who made the excursions on boats. Others walked across the toll-free bridge.

In 1894 the philanthropist Thomas Palmer deeded Log Cabin Farm, located on Woodward, six miles north of the Detroit River, to the city. This land was beautified and converted into Palmer Park. The park was easily accessible by public transportation.

In 1890 the city purchased twenty-four and one-half acres on the west side as the site for Clark Park. Other neighborhood parks were also developed. In 1900 the city could boast of a total of 926 acres in its modern system of parks.

Humanitarian efforts and larger appropriations for the Board of Health combined to give Detroiters better medical care. In 1900 only one hospital, the United States Marine Hospital, was maintained by public funds. This hospital, which received its first patients in 1857, was established by Congress to care for seamen on the Great Lakes. It later extended its services to disabled servicemen.

Other Detroit hospitals were established and maintained by private contributions. At the outbreak of the Civil War Detroit's sole private hospital was St. Mary's, conducted by the Sisters of Charity. In 1859, however, a contribution by Walter Harper assured funds for the hospital that was to bear his name. During the Civil War the trustees negotiated for a military hospital which was authorized in 1863 and was constructed during the next year. Many disabled Michigan troops were sent to the hospital for convalescence. In

December, 1865 the facilities of the hospital, renamed Harper Hospital, were made available to Detroit residents.

Grace Hospital originally served homeopathic practitioners. Although homeopathic physicians and surgeons had long planned a hospital, construction was assured in 1886 when James McMillan contributed $100,000. John S. Newberry later matched the McMillan grant.

The Detroit hospitals promoted medical knowledge. Clinics and dispensaries marked the beginning of the city's contemporary out-patient programs. By 1900 the training schools for nurses had helped to make nursing a recognized profession.

An alert Board of Health recommended policies and proposed city ordinances to promote public health. Until 1880 the city department was primarily concerned with the purification of water, sewage disposal, the enforcement of quarantines, and the recording of vital statistics. After 1880 the Board took more stringent steps to assure adequate meat inspection, pure milk, and better ventilation in public buildings. Many of the city ordinances preceded similar legislation at the state level. The Board of Health also undertook a vigorous program of health education. By 1900 many citizens gave their support to programs of tuberculosis control.

In 1900 Detroit's death rate was 14.04 per thousand population. This rate was well below that of many large cities. Infant and child mortality, however, remained high. Some 1,149 of the 4,934 deaths recorded in 1900 were of infants under one year of age, and one-half of the deaths were of individuals under the age of thirty. Contagious diseases took a heavy toll. In 1900 diphtheria claimed 617 lives and scarlet fever 343.

The charity movement was sustained primarily by the religious organizations. The social program of the Roman Catholic Church was the broadest. The Sisters of Charity

and other orders drew upo
expand an impressive socia
Providence Hospital had
Providence, established in
women and abandoned child
for the orphans and the ag

Protestant churches also e
unfortunate. Often projects
denominations. St. Luke's H
phanage was established by
Episcopal). Detroit Luthera
located in Royal Oak. On oc
interdenominational. In 1868
outlined its plans for the Wom
Home, the predecessor of ou
pital.

The small Jewish population
sistance to its members in ne
arrived immigrants were giver
Society, an adjunct of Temple
services.

Non-denominational organizat
new community spirit. The Y.N
existence in Detroit since 1864,
house" for charity drives. In th
nastic and recreational facilities
The Y.W.C.A., established at
recreational facilities and gave a:
young women.

Private charity organizations, of
meet all the new social and econo
the growing urban complexity. T
gave assistance to widows, ophans
the poor who could not be reached
The new concept of help for the

ments to m
ernment w

In 1899
ried coupl
wives who
band was
six single
given assi
of unemp
because o

Wayne
relief pro
enlarged.
illness.

In the
fare prol
majority
normal c
lived und
cities.

Cautio
ing. Mea
the late
own. Th
—wages,
would in
standarc
run, in
living in
the bro
sion of
for rap
howeve
to mee

A survey undertaken in 1883 revealed that the average daily wage of male skilled and unskilled workers was $1.74. Only eighty-two out of a total of 8,611 workers received between $4.00 and $7.00 per day. A total of 224 received ninety cents or less per day. Some 5,229 men averaged between $1.00 and $2.40 daily. The variations within each occupation are noticeable. The daily wage of barbers ranged from $1.15 to $2.35. The wage of butchers ranged from eighty-five cents to $2.00.

The daily average wage for unskilled laborers was $1.45. The skilled, of course, fared better. The average wage of a bricklayer was $2.81.[8] In many of the occupations twelve hours constituted the standard working day. Many of the workers, however, had succeeded in obtaining the ten-hour day or less. Unfortunately, these differentials were not indicated. The intervals of unemployment, also, are unknown.

The majority of city employees received an annual salary. The Superintendent of the Police Department and the Super-

---

[8] The average daily wages for selected occupations is as follows:

Bartenders	$1.31
Cabinetmaker	1.68
Carpenters	1.59
Clerks and salesmen	1.92
Cooks	1.67
Gardeners	1.15
Hackdrivers	1.45
Janitors	1.25
Machinists	2.57
Masons	2.56
Millwrights	2.62
Painters	1.99
Photographers	2.50
Plasterers	2.40
Shoemakers	1.69
Printers	1.63
Teamsters	1.50
Wagonmakers	1.99

Michigan Bureau of Labor, *Annual Report*, 1, pp. 90-91.

intendent of the Detroit Schools were the recipients of the highest salary—$4,000. Patrolmen were paid $750.[9]

Wages for women were usually lower than those of men. In 1883 the average daily wage of 503 women was seventy-eight cents. Forty-five women received forty-five cents or less per day. Only eleven women averaged $1.75 or more as a daily wage. The highest average wage, $1.07, was paid to milliners.

In 1892 a study of 2,102 female employees, of whom 276 were married, revealed that the average age was 24.7 years. The average number of years employed in the same establishment was 3.6; the average number of months employed was 10.8; and the average number of hours employed per day was 9.8. One-third of the women reported regular savings.

In 1896 the working day for girls in the tobacco establishments varied from nine to ten hours. Employment in tobacco factories seemed to have a favored position. Employment in suits, pants, and corset establishments was also desirable. Laundry work had a low status, and the sorting of rags was the least desirable.

Of the 1,110 girls employed in the tobacco industry, 1,094 lived at home. Most of the girls worked to supplement the family income. One girl worked primarily to take music lessons; another labored merely to "pay for a watch."

Newcomers, except in depression years, apparently found employment without difficulty. Even non-English speaking

---

[9] Other representative salaries are as follows:

City Treasurer	$3,000
Assistant to the Treasurer	1,500
City Clerk	2,500
City Engineer	2,500
	1,600
Janitor, City Hall	1,034
Meter Tester	660
Police Sergeant	900
Captain, Fire Department	950
Lieutenant, Fire Department	850

Ibid., p. 176.

immigrants were quickly absorbed in the labor market. Employers frequently reported a shortage of skilled laborers.

A survey undertaken in 1892 comprising sixty-one industries and 5,379 male laborers revealed an average working day of 10.2 hours for 10.9 months per year. Labor turnover, obviously, was not frequent, since the average employee had been with the same establishment for 13.6 years. About one-half the married men owned their own homes, and approximately one-third of these had no mortgages or other home debts. The average monthly savings was $6.98.

Two representative budgets throw some light on the standards of living for skilled workers in 1892:[10]

[10] Michigan Bureau of Labor, *Annual Report*, X, pp. 1043-45.

	Laborer's Budget	Carpenter's Budget
Bread stuffs	$ 1.02	$ 2.05
Butter	.78	1.51
Milk	.67	1.19
Eggs	.48	.18
Sugar	.86	1.13
Coffee	.35	.60
Meat	1.57	1.82
Poultry	.57	.80
Fish	.54	.25
Fruits and vegetables	.85	3.07
Fuel and light	3.58	.64
Clothing	.25	2.75
Boots and shoes		2.50
Medical	.35	1.05
Rent	11.00	10.00
Furniture	4.40	
Literature	.02	
Tobacco	.80	
Amusements		2.25
Taxes and insurance	4.05	1.80
Carfare	.10	11.10
Postage	.12	
Sundries	1.33	
Total Expenditures	$34.14	$44.75
Earnings	27.00	52.00
Excess of Expenditures over Earnings	7.14	7.25 Savings
Month — November, 1891		Month — July, 1892

After the Civil War labor gradually became a significant force. A number of labor philosophies were developed. These ranged from the rigid and narrow doctrinaire to the highly pragmatic. The most successful movements, however, were identified with the previous and contemporary American traditions.

There was some organized activity, of course, even before 1861. Although members of the various mechanics' societies often discussed economic problems, these societies were primarily benevolent in character. In 1848 the printers, informally organized for a number of years, established the Typographical Union, the first of Detroit's trade unions. In 1860 the iron molders founded a highly successful union. By 1864 the machinists, blacksmiths, cigar makers, carpenters, and operative plasterers had also organized.

Much credit for their expansion should be given to Richard Trevellick, who was very active in enrolling members in the various trade unions and whose appeals for the support of labor activities reached large audiences. This English-born labor leader was also identified with the eight-hour day movement and other national liberal reforms. He maintained very friendly relations with political leaders and helped to give labor a degree of political stature. In fact, it was no uncommon occurrence to find working men nominated for office by each of the major parties.

The Detroit Trades Assembly, the first central trade union association in Michigan, was formed in 1864 primarily through Trevellick's influence. This organization had a particular appeal at the time, since wages during the Civil War usually did not keep pace with the increase in prices. The Assembly, which achieved a membership of 5,000, demanded larger wages and a shorter working week. In 1872 the Assembly began to decline because of factional and personality differences. The Panic of 1873 brought about its official death.

During this period of partial decadence in trade unions, the Knights of Labor appeared. This society, founded at Philadelphia in 1869 by Uriah Stephens, encouraged the inclusion of all workers in one large union. Although the original plans suggested a secret fraternal order, by 1881 the organization had abandoned secrecy and was stressing cooperative and broad programs of economic and social reform. The administrative character of the Knights of Labor gave considerable freedom of action to the primary, or cell, unit. Strikes were discouraged as weapons of action, but they were not entirely prohibited.

The Knights of Labor reached Detroit in 1879, when Charles Litchman, a shoemaker from the East, came to the city for the purpose of encouraging members of this trade to join the organization. The scheduled meeting was never held, but Litchman enlisted the support of several Detroit individuals, including Joseph Labadie, a printer of unusual literary talents, who soon became one of the outstanding champions of the labor cause.

By the middle 1880's, the Knights had enrolled a large Detroit membership. Yet, by 1890 the Detroit organization had become virtually extinct for a number of reasons: quarrels among rival personalities produced the inevitable factionalism; the few cooperative ventures were not successful; the union failed at the state level to secure many promised reforms. Even more fundamental as a source of friction was the issue of political action. One group desired the Knights to serve as a nucleus for a liberal third party, and varying degrees of semi-official endorsement were given to the several third parties which flourished, successively, during the decade of the 1880's. Another group, more conservative, frowned upon political flirtations. Controversies often ensued. After the Haymarket bombing in Chicago, the order was split further along conservative-liberal lines.

Finally, trade union people began to question the effectiveness of the entire program.

The contributions of the Knights to labor, however, were many. The educational program, especially the emphasis upon social and economic problems, filled a real void. The foundation of the labor press can be traced to its journals. It was a training school for many later constructive labor efforts. It brought Detroit and upstate labor leaders together.

The activities of the Knights of Labor did not prevent other labor groups from functioning. Although the majority of trade union men in Detroit were at one time or another affiliated with the Knights, the degree of sympathy for the organization was, in many respects, very nominal. Many trade union people were frankly suspicious of the Knights, and in 1881 formed the Detroit Council of Trades and Labor Unions. This Council was made up of representatives from each of the leading trade unions in the city. It took a very active interest in all problems affecting workers and on various occasions even endorsed candidates for political office. In 1888 it assumed a major role in bringing about the formation of the Michigan Federation of Labor.

Many Detroit unions, which had general programs and goals similar to those of the American Federation of Labor, retained their separate identities. The railway brotherhoods were among the most important. The Grand International Brotherhood of Locomotive Engineers traces its origin to the formation of the Brotherhood of the Footboard in Detroit in 1863.

The trade unions acted on the principle of aiding labor to secure higher wages and better working conditions under a flourishing system of capitalism. Ordinarily the agents of the unions negotiated without resorting to strikes. Issues over wages, hours of labor, and recognition of the closed shop were among the major causes of the strikes that did occur. Although the Detroit Council was never the adjunct of a party, it often endorsed candidates. It was highly successful, moreover, in cooperating with organizations that championed reform in city government.

There was, of course, a steady rise in church membership with the increase in population. Immigrants contributed to the Roman Catholic gain. In 1882 approximately 43,500 Detroit residents were members of the Roman Catholic faith. Bishop Caspar Henry Borgess (1870-1887) successfully initiated many programs including the enlargement of the parochial school system.

The majority of Jewish newcomers were also immigrants. Before 1890 Detroit's Jewish population was largely of German-speaking background. Temple Beth El was the sole Reform congregation. The other synagogues adhered to a Conservative or Orthodox position.

Virtually all Protestant denominations were represented in Detroit. Comparative figures for church membership are, of course, approximations. In 1880 among the Protestant denominations the Episcopalians had the largest Detroit membership. The Presbyterians, Lutherans, Methodists, and Congregationalists followed in the order indicated. Many other denominations, although well represented, had a relatively small membership. In 1900 Detroit had 190 churches of which thirty-two were Roman Catholic, thirty-two Methodist-Episcopal, twenty-five Lutheran, twenty-three Episcopal, seventeen Baptist, sixteen Presbyterian, nine Congregational, nine German Evangelical, and four Jewish. Another eighteen churches represented Protestant denominations with quite small memberships.

By 1900 each church had modified or enlarged its program to meet urban requirements. Frequently a portion of the church building was used as a hall or community center. Churches sponsored lectures and staged plays they considered to be more elevating than commercial entertainment. Separate programs were sponsored by young peoples' societies and other auxiliary groups. The voice of the clergy also remained important when Detroiters debated civic and social issues.

More and more leisure time was given to organizations. Fraternal orders, of course, are associated even with the early history of Detroit. Masonry in Detroit dates back to 1764. After the Civil War, however, the number of fraternal orders in Detroit multiplied rapidly. Ethnic and religious social organizations were also numerous. By 1900 the professional and occupational organizations were legion. Yachting and other recreational activities also needed organization. The serious side of life was not neglected, however. Study clubs, debating societies, and literary clubs flourished among all economic classes.

The theater reflected the maturing and sophisticated middle-class life of Detroit. After 1880 modern theaters with spacious lobbies and good acoustics presented the stars of Broadway. Maxine Eliot, Sarah Bernhardt, and other prominent names elevated the stage to the status of culture. In 1900 Detroit had seven theaters, including one given over to the variety show or vaudeville performances.

Good editing, good reporting, and good writing enabled several Detroit dailies to dominate journalism. In 1900 the *Free Press* was Detroit's leading morning paper. The other major dailies were of more recent origin. The *Tribune,* also a morning paper, was owned by James E. Scripps. The *News,* the leading afternoon and evening journal, was founded by Scripps in 1873. In 1883 Floyd Breeze founded the *Detroit Evening Journal* which became the chief rival of the *News.*

All of these papers gave Detroit residents excellent news coverage. Their readers were kept well informed on local events. In fact, collectively, the press virtually molded the pattern of Detroit's civic consciousness. Dramatic critics and book-review editors kept readers abreast of cultural developments.

The expansion of school facilities was one of the outstanding contributions of the municipal government. In 1890 approximately 23,000 of the 63,000 children of school age were enrolled. At the close of the century school attendance was 35,000. The system employed 900 teachers.

The introduction of evening schools and the establishment of an ungraded school for truants were among the unusual features of the Detroit system. In 1895 a new Central High School was authorized and plans were made for two additional neighborhood high schools—Eastern and Western.

Until 1881 the schools were supervised by a Board of Education elected on a ward basis. Charges of extravagance and favoritism resulted in pressure in 1881 for a small board elected at large. The new body came under attack for its neglect of schools in the recently developed areas. Finally, in 1889 the plan of ward representation was restored.

In reality, basic educational policies were presented by the Superintendent of Schools. Between 1865 and 1900 four capable superintendents—Duane Doty, John M. B. Sill, William Robinson, and Wales Martindale—headed the Detroit system. Under their leadership the Detroit public schools became known for their excellence.

Music came to play a prominent part in Detroit's cultural life. All of the ladies' singing societies increased their membership and enlarged their programs. The Concordia Society, formed in 1866, sponsored the production of light operas. In 1872 a Detroit Symphony Orchestra was organized with forty members.

By 1890 Detroit was the home of many bands. Throughout the 1890's the band concert was an eagerly awaited neighborhood function during the summer weeks. Concerts at Belle Isle were unusually well attended. The musical numbers ranged from the very popular to the semiclassic.

At a Belle Isle concert on July 4, 1898, the audience heard "Remember the Maine" and Wagnerian selections.

The increase in the number of private conservatories of music by 1900 is evidence of broader cultural interests, greater wealth, and more leisure. The number of private teachers of music was large. Schools of dancing were also numerous.

In 1875 the Detroit Art Association was organized by several of the city's prominent artists. The Association sponsored several well-attended exhibits. Its leaders hoped for the establishment of a permanent art gallery, but their ideas and goals proved to be premature.

In 1883 a very exciting and successful art exhibition stimulated interest in a permanent art institute. Art enthusiasts conducted a drive to raise $40,000. Senator Thomas Palmer led the list of contributions with a donation of $10,000. As a result of the successful campaign, a permanent building, located at Jefferson near Hastings, was opened to the public in 1888. It remained the home of the Detroit Museum of Art until 1927, when the city government, which had begun to support the museum in 1919, completed the $4,000,000 edifice on Woodward.

After the Civil War Detroit's growth brought many physical changes. The downtown commercial area was rapidly transformed. In 1865 commerce centered around the crossing of Jefferson and Woodward and the east and west streets south of Jefferson. This area developed as a business section as an outgrowth of the days when business activity was related to river traffic. Very gradually before the close of the century, establishments began to move north and Woodward Avenue became the established "Main Street." The presence of the major retail stores on Woodward indicated that more Detroiters were moving to newly developed northern portions of the city "out Woodward."

By 1900 the retail stores in the downtown area had given way to the new emporia. Department stores served a more elite trade. Other large establishments sold to the working-man at lower prices. These stores had frequent bargain sales. Specialty shops sold at a variety of price levels. Confectioneries and bakeries were numerous. An outstanding feature of the downtown area was the presence of many artisans' shops. The increase in number during the decade of the 1890's was phenomenal. Furriers, jewelers, and gentlemen tailors were numerous and rendered services that reflected an increase in wealth. The far-from-insignificant wholesale trade remained in the heart of the business area of 1865. Professional men also had their downtown offices. Attorneys were clustered on lower Woodward. Physicians with downtown offices were usually specialists rather than general practitioners.

Woodward and Jefferson avenues were not given over exclusively to business. At the very edge of the commercial section each street became residential. Some of the most expensive homes in Detroit were within two miles of the downtown business district.

By 1900 public buildings had acquired a greater elegance. City Hall, on Woodward Avenue opposite Cadillac Square, was completed in 1872. The spacious County Building was constructed during the 1890's. Size was also stressed in the Union Depot on West Fort Street, which was opened to the public in 1893. Hotels reflected a new elegance. The Russell House, located at Woodward and Cadillac Square, ranked among the "plush" hotels of the entire Middle West. All of the newer hotels—in their guest rooms, dining rooms, and menus—emphasized an up-to-dateness in place of the older and relatively plain Midwestern practices.

The physical changes and their significance were astutely observed by a contemporary journalist:

All the way along Woodward to the Grand Circus are great establishments doing an immense volume of business.

The character of the business transacted below the Campus on Woodward has changed materially from what it was, but it has not deteriorated in the least. It has simply been an expansion of trade. Probably just as much business, or even more, is now transacted every day below the city hall as in 1883, but it is not the same trend of trade. . . .

Not only has business stretched out along Detroit's principal thoroughfare during the past 12 years, but it has also expanded into the main arteries like Michigan Avenue, Grand River, Gratiot, and Monroe, and to-day there are commercial houses on the streets named which are doing a business fully equal to that done by any of the houses, which, in 1883, believed that the only location for successful trading was on Woodward-ave., between State-st., and Jefferson-ave., and the nearer the latter intersection the better. . . .

The removal of the immense clothing establishment of J. L. Hudson from Woodward-ave., to Gratiot created an entirely new trade center, which has developed to a wonderful and correspondingly gratifying degree. The locality had previously been devoted to residence and church purposes with a fringe of the small clan of tradesmen, but to-day it is one of the most bustling and thriving localities to be found in the city and furnishes a connecting link between Woodward and Gratiot-ave. proper.

The latter thoroughfare has developed in late years fully as rapidly as any of the others and some of the largest and most handsome modern business blocks are to be found on each side of old Gratiot.

Customers of these firms are no longer confined to their immediate localities, but, with improved street car service, universal transfers and attractive bargains, their stores are thronged daily by people of every nationality, indicating that they came from every portion of the city, including the suburbs."

---

[11] *The Detroit Journal*, Thirteenth Anniversary Edition.

CHAPTER IV

The Automotive City (1901-1945)

In 1900 Detroit was at the threshold of an unprecedented industrial expansion. Between 1900 and 1910 the population increased from 285,000 to 465,000. It was doubled in the next decade to 993,000, placing the city in the position of the fourth largest in the United States. A tremendous increase during the boom 1920's brought Detroit's population to 1,568,000 by 1930. Although the gains during the depression decade of the 1930's were insignificant, by 1940 Detroit had a population of 1,623,000.

The automotive industry, of course, was the major force behind this growth. The "horseless carriage" transformed Detroit into a leading manufacturing city. Detroit became a city that could assure unusual economic opportunities to all.

The following figures illustrate the phenomenal increase in employment opportunities as a result of the automobile industry. In 1908 the automotive industry in the city gave employment to only 7,200 workers. In 1909 some 17,000 were employed by the automotive manufacturers. By 1915 the figure had increased to 81,000. In 1916, even prior to America's entrance into World War I, the industry employed some 120,000 persons.

Along with the upsurge of employment came a startling increase in wages. In 1913 the average daily wage was $2.60. By 1918 this had increased to $4.72, then to $5.30 the following year. Detroit was elevated to the rank of the boom city of the nation.

Many reasons have been advanced for the rise of the infant automotive industry in Detroit. The city already was an important center for the manufacture of carriages, wagons, bicycles, and marine engines. The availability of a pool of skilled and semi-skilled mechanics was another favorable factor. Yet, this was true of other cities, for in the pioneering phase of the industry, they, too, were engaged in the manufacture of automobiles—offering inducements equal to those of Detroit.

Undoubtedly it was the chance role of personalities that ultimately made Detroit the focal point of the automotive industry. Several of the city's pioneers moved forward rapidly and their progress was the determining factor in making Detroit the automotive capital of the world.

Detroit's automotive growth began with Ransom E. Olds of Lansing, Michigan, whose father manufactured gasoline engines. By the early 1890's Olds was keenly interested in the new horseless carriage. By 1898 he was certain that a good market awaited a manufacturer of a standardized gasoline-driven automobile. Like so many who eventually attained success in the automotive world, Olds found it difficult to secure financial backing.

In 1899 Olds had sufficient capital to establish a factory in Detroit. It was, in many respects, an assembly plant, for Olds contracted with expert Detroit machinists to produce the parts for his one-cylinder car. Subcontractors of Olds soon found themselves pioneers in a new and exciting industry.

The Olds automobile immediately sold beyond all expectations. In 1901 the company produced 1,500 of the 7,000 motor vehicles built in the United States. The Olds was the first car to be successfully manufactured, and its success focused the attention of automotive people upon Detroit. In 1902, when the Olds factory was destroyed by fire, Ransom Olds removed his plant to Lansing but continued to receive many parts from Detroit. The loss of this plant, however, was no great blow to Detroit's automotive prestige, for other manufacturers were entering the field.

Henry Ford soon brought even greater automotive fame to Detroit. In the 1890's Ford was one of many men who built "home-made" cars. In 1899 the Detroit Automobile Company, the forerunner of the Cadillac Automobile Company, employed Ford as its manager upon the basis of his automotive reputation. This relationship proved far from satisfactory, so in 1901 Ford organized his own concern, the Henry Ford Motor Company.

From 1901 until 1903 Ford achieved only moderate success. Then in 1903 his company was reorganized and renamed the Ford Motor Company. Sales of inexpensive and moderately priced models were satisfactory. By 1909 Ford stabilized the policy of the company by confining production exclusively to a standard low price car, the Model T, that would appeal to both urban and rural motorists. Some 18,600 cars were sold during the first year of this new policy. The Ford facilities could not expand with sufficient speed to keep pace with the flood of orders. In 1914 the Highland Park Plant was completed. Here, two innovations of real significance were introduced almost simultaneously. The first, the minimum five-dollar-a-day wage, soon revolutionized wage scales throughout the entire nation. The second, the introduction of the mass-production assembly principle was a major technological phenomenon of this century.

In 1914 Ford made 308,000 automobiles. Two years later the number rose astronomically to 785,000. By 1927, when production of the Model T ended, 15,000,000 cars of this design had been manufactured.

The increase in employment indicates why many Americans associated Detroit's growth with Ford. In 1908 the Ford Motor Company employed 450 workers. In 1913 the number of employees reached 14,000. Three years later the total of Ford employees was 36,000.

The revolutionary practices inaugurated by Ford were, almost of necessity, followed by the majority of the successful competitors. Ford, however, remained among the leaders. The huge market necessitated a constant expansion of facilities, facilities which did not become adequate until the River Rouge Plant, projected in 1914, was completed during the 1920's. In 1919, Ford completed the process of purchasing the stock of his original associates; the concern became a family company. Stock was not sold publicly until 1957.

Many men of later prominence were associated with the early history of the Ford Motor Company. Engines for the Ford were manufactured by John and Horace Dodge, who were also leading stockholders in the Ford Company. In 1914 Ford purchased their shares. The Dodge brothers then established their own company to produce the well-known Dodge automobile. James Couzens, another early Ford partner, was in many respects the business genius of the Ford enterprise. Unlike the Dodges, Couzens retired from the automotive field after he sold his interests in the Ford Motor Company and soon entered politics.

Public interest in Henry Ford began to match the interest shown in his automobile. To many, his meteoric rise was a symbol of success for the individual of modest origin. Ford was born on a farm in Dearborn. Although he possessed most of the rural virtues, he came to believe that much of the drudgery on the farm could be avoided and the standard of living raised through technology. In the later years of his life, Ford was able to implement many of the ideas acquired on the farm during his youth.

In 1879, at the age of twenty-nine, Ford left the farm for Detroit. There he received excellent apprentice training as a mechanic. On one occasion he repaired watches to supplement his income. He also found time to attend a business college.

In 1893, already in early middle age, Ford was employed as a night engineer by the Detroit Edison Company. He became interested in the automobile. For five years he experimented with his own models. When he became superintendent of the Detroit Automobile Company, he severed his connections with the Edison Company.

The five-dollar-a-day wage scale enhanced Ford's popularity. He established a company personnel program that combined features of rigid paternalism with welfare programs.

Ford identified himself with two crusades. He endorsed prohibition and the peace cause. In 1915 he headed a self-financed peace delegation to Europe. This highly publicized venture brought both praise and sharp ridicule.

Ford gradually emerged as a personality with political stature. Each of the major parties sought his support. In 1918 Ford was the Democratic nominee for United States Senator. In the November contest Ford lost to Truman H. Newberry, his Republican rival, by a very narrow margin.

The 1918 campaign was Ford's last official venture as a candidate. After World War I he identified himself with the Republican Party. During the early 1920's his name was mentioned frequently as a presidential prospect. It was also during the early 1920's that Ford authorized the publication of articles, with strong anti-Semitic undertones, in his *Dearborn Independent.* He ended these attacks, however, with a public retraction. The Ford press conferences, however, continued to make "news." Although Ford inaugurated many semi-paternalistic projects for his employees, he resisted unionism. The Ford Motor Company was the last of the automotive giants to recognize the United Automobile Workers (U.A.W.) as the bargaining agent for employees.

A host of other Detroit automotive pioneers also contributed to the growth of the industry. Although the Detroit

Automobile Company collapsed in 1902, it served as the nucleus for the successful Cadillac Automobile Company. This concern was fortunate in receiving the services of Henry Leland. Under his direction the Cadillac soon acquired a national reputation. The Cadillac, at an early date, emphasized luxury features in its campaign to increase an interest in motoring.

In 1903 Detroit became the home of the Packard Motor Company. Earlier models had been manufactured in Warren, Ohio, since 1899. Truman Newberry, Henry Joy and other wealthy Detroiters invested in the company and procured its relocation. The Packard almost immediately captured a large percentage of the "higher price" market.

By 1903 Olds, Ford, Cadillac, and Packard—four names still famous in the automotive industry—were associated with Detroit. The list of major manufacturers was rapidly enlarged. In 1903 the Hupp Automobile Company began production of a popular medium-priced automobile in Detroit. In the following year Roy Chapin, an early Olds employee, assumed the leadership in the formation of the Hudson Motor Company. J. L. Hudson, a leading Detroit merchant, helped to finance the concern.

The list of "graveyard" manufacturers in Detroit is also lengthy. Many companies were directed by men who lacked the combined mechanical and business acumen required for success in the pioneer automotive field. Other companies were inadequately financed. In many instances, the initial capital was not sufficient to provide for the necessary minimum expenditures for advertising and adjustments to the rapid technological changes.

Successful Detroit companies produced for a national market. They manufactured automobiles that could be operated in rural and urban areas; their products could be sold in both mountainous and flat lands. Strange as it may seem, few among the many automotive pioneers grasped the significance of the national market.

Only a small percentage of the manufacturers knew how to sell, in a highly competitive industry, the successful development techniques for advertising and distribution. They were well aware of the importance of a network of dealerships.

The major automotive companies in Detroit expanded largely from their profits. Successful concerns lowered their unit costs of production and increased their volume of sales. These procedures, over a period of a few years, enabled the companies to enlarge their dealerships and to promote rapid technological developments. Detroit companies emphasized safety. They helped to change the automobile from a fad for the few to a necessity sold to millions of Americans for transportation. The Detroit magnets helped to elevate the industry to a "Big Business" status.

In the early years of the automobile, motoring had a limited impact. Ownership of an automobile was restricted to enthusiasts. Motorists were, of necessity, men of some means, for the mere cost of ownership and maintenance tended to exclude those in the lower-income brackets.

Speed was greatly restricted on the streets of Detroit. In 1903 the city, by ordinance, established a maximum speed of eight miles per hour on the majority of highways. The city also required a municipal license for each automobile; later Michigan made the state license mandatory.

Detroit had its first automobile show in 1902. Exhibitors included many from out of state. This indicated the beginning of specialized services such as sales. The rental of storage facilities was also common by 1903. Many of the companies selling automobile supplies continued to merchandise other products. Automotive retailers sold auxiliary equipment that would be regarded today as standard.

By 1908, Detroit fully appreciated the significance of the industry. The automobile became a leading and choice topic of conversation in business circles. Detroiters finally sensed the importance of the city's role as the capital of the automotive industry.

By 1916 Detroit had won recognition as a great manufacturing city. Between 1915 and 1916 industrial production rose from $600,000 to $900,000,000. In this one-year interval the value of automotive products doubled from $300,000,000 to $600,000,000. Yet the manufacture of stoves, furnaces, paints, pharmaceutical products, chemicals, and tobacco remained important. In 1916 establishments in the city produced 1,000,000 cigars a day.

Although American participation in World War I officially dates from the declaration of war on April 6, 1917, the impact of the struggle upon the economy and the psychology of the people in Detroit could be clearly seen as early as the summer of 1915. The industrial products of the city were in great demand. Many of the companies undertook elaborate programs of plant expansion. The possibility of involvement in the war also became a much debated subject.

Detroit's great industrial potential was clearly recognized after the United States became a belligerent. The Ford Motor Company produced boats to serve as submarine chasers. Lincoln Motor devoted its huge energies primarily to aviation. The Packard Motor Company also manufactured aircraft. Many of the newly developed tanks were produced in Detroit. Although the automotive industry was never asked to abandon its civilian output, by the close of the war war materials comprised the larger portion of its immense productivity.

Approximately 65,000 men and women from the Detroit area were enrolled in the armed forces. The several draft registrations were carried out with very little difficulty.

Many citizens volunteered their services to assist in the labors of these boards.

Many of the Detroit men who were sent overseas were attached to the Thirty-second and Eighty-fifth Divisions. The Thirty-second Division was comprised of Michigan and Wisconsin guardsmen. It was the first American division to set foot on German soil, and it became a part of the Army of Occupation in Germany. Its insignia, a flying red arrow with a red crossbar in the middle, signified its achievement in being the first to break the Hindenburg Line. The Eighty-fifth Division was made up largely of Michigan and Wisconsin draftees. It trained at Camp Custer, a cantonment near Battle Creek, Michigan, and was nicknamed the Custer Division. One of its regiments, the Three Hundred and Thirty-ninth, largely composed of Detroiters, was sent to Russia, where it remained through the very severe winter of 1918 and 1919. For this service it become known as the Polar Bears. The medical profession of Detroit furnished the personnel for Harper Base Hospital Unit Number 17 and the Detroit College of Medicine for Base Hospital Unit Number 36.

The war goals were explained to Detroiters in well-organized and well-directed drives. Volunteer speakers who received information on the American objectives from the Committee of Public Information spoke in many public places, including theaters. These speakers, known as four-minute men, were trained to present their messages briefly and to the point.

Five major drives were undertaken to sell war bonds. In 1917 Detroiters subscribed $42,290,000 to the first Liberty Bond Drive; in 1918 $184,000,000 was subscribed in three subsequent drives. Detroit citizens were also generous in their contributions to the Red Cross, Y.M.C.A., Salvation Army, Knights of Columbus, Jewish Welfare Board, and other organizations that aided men and women in the armed forces.

The growth of Detroit did not bring immediate changes in the municipal voting. The Democrats remained strong in city elections. The majority of mayoralty campaigns were decided by very narrow margins. Between 1900 and 1918 the Republicans and Democrats virtually outwitted each other in mayoralty contests.

Pingree had given prestige to the office of mayor. His immediate successors lacked his stature. He had endorsed and defended his own programs before an electorate. Ironically, both Democratic and Republican nominees for mayor in subsequent elections pledged themselves to many of Pingree's reforms. All promised a rapid solution to the problem of streetcar service. No mayor, however, successfully implemented these compaign promises.

Many aldermen failed to understand the problem of a modern and growing city, and too frequently represented specific local interests. The Royal Ark Association, the spokesman for liquor interests, endorsed aldermen who opposed further restrictions upon saloons. Charges of favoritism and even "graft" were numerous, but many of these indictments were dismissed as part of "politics."

Ward and precinct organizations played a major role in municipal elections. They did an unusually effective job in securing a maximum turnout among their followers on crucial election days. Very often they helped to turn the tide against reforms, including prohibition and woman suffrage.

The rapid growth of Detroit after 1908 gradually weakened these organizations in two respects. First, new voting precincts were created, in which political organization could not be easily attained. Frequently, newcomers were even indifferent to other than major municipal issues. Secondly, the frequent neighborhood transition caused a realignment in politics that brought advantages to the Republicans.

Early in the century the Republicans tended to hold a slight margin in the general elections for county, state, and national offices. Wayne County, because of the Republican strength outside of Detroit, usually was found in the Republican columns. By 1916, because of Republican gains, it was difficult for a Democrat to be elected to a county office.

The problems growing out of the phenomenal increase in population created sentiment for charter revision. Considerable dissatisfaction was expressed concerning the Board of Estimates which, in practice, served as an upper house. Many citizens also believed that the Board of Aldermen was dominated largely by neighborhood interests. Charges of local patronage and influence were repeatedly made. In 1916 the electorate finally approved the abolition of the cumbersome Board of Estimates. On June 25, 1918, a new charter won approval by a large margin.

The new charter embodied unusual features for a city as large as Detroit. The large forty-two-member council, comprised of members representing individual wards, was replaced by a nine-member council chosen at large. The power of the mayor was spelled out in detail and enlarged. All of the officials, including judges, were to be chosen on a non-partisan basis. The Board of Education became a small body of seven chosen at large on a non-partisan basis.

The success of the charter revision was the result of several factors. Strong support from the press was most helpful. The Scripps' papers were in the vanguard of municipal reform. No Detroit newspaper was entirely critical of reform. Officially each party had endorsed a general program for municipal reform. Civic leaders, including jurists and other prominent professional men, advocated basic changes in the pattern of government. Specific organizations, including the Citizens' League, also added strength to the reform cause.

The great immediate demand for additional urban services during World War I convinced many voters that partisan politics and ward representation must go. A segment of
the population feared a possible delay in school construction under the existing charter. Others were disgruntled with
the ineffectiveness of the transportation system. Very few
could defend the existing system. Piecemeal changes received little support from critics, who reminded the electorate of the basic failure of the previous minor reforms. In the
last analysis vested interests were forced to defend the old
charter with arguments of loss of neighborhood representation and possible rule by a clique interest without party
responsibility.

Undoubtedly, many endorsed the new charter because it
spelled "reform." To these individuals the changes in the
pattern of government were in line with the traditions of
progressivism. Many saw the charter as the basis for more
drastic reforms, including municipal ownership of the street
railways and other utilities. Finally, many Democrats sensed
the slow trend toward the Republicans. These Democrats
apparently saw an opportunity to secure election to office
if a non-partisan government were approved.

The transition in government was orderly. James Couzens,
heralded as a second Pingree, easily won the contest for
mayor. Five of the new council members had served in
the old council. The new body was regarded as reform-
minded.

The first mayor under the new charter perhaps typified
the new hopes. James Couzens was well known to Detroiters
as a Ford "partner." Canadian-born Couzens had come to
Detroit at an early age and worked as a railroad helper.
Early in this century he became the bookkeeper for the Mal-
comson Coal Company. He also was the bookkeeper for
the Ford Motor Company after his employer invested
heavily in the new company. Couzens increased his invest-

ments in the automotive concern and served as Ford's financial adviser. He sold his shares to Ford and became one of Detroit's richest men, later turning to politics. He served efficiently as police commissioner before he won election as mayor. He successfully fought for the municipal ownership of the streetcar system. It was Couzens who would not allow the city government to retract its stand on municipal ownership.

Couzens was appointed to the Senate of the United States by Governor Alex Groesbeck. He was re-elected in several contests. In the Roosevelt era he consistently supported the New Deal. This support apparently contributed to his defeat in the Republican senatorial primary contest in 1936.

During the early 1920's, Detroit, largely because of the leadership of Mayor Couzens, made a final decision concerning public transportation. In 1919 the electorate, by a narrow margin, defeated a bond issue for the construction of a municipally owned street railway system. In the next year, however, the bond issue won the necessary sixty percent approval, and construction began almost immediately. In 1921 the city was authorized to purchase the Detroit United Railways System. Negotiations were rapidly completed to make the entire system city-owned. In 1932 the private bus lines were also purchased by the municipal Detroit Street Railways (D. S. R.).

In the 1920's, Detroit became the boom city of all boom cities. Except for the brief recession of 1921 employment was high. By 1927 the population had increased from 993,000 to 1,500,000. In 1910 the assessed valuation of property was $377,000,000. In 1927 the assessed valuation was $3,394,000,000.

This new economic tempo was paced by the automotive industry, for during this period the automobile had virtually become a necessity. The increasing popularity of the automobile was undoubtedly without parallel. In fact, the automobile, because of the unusual importance of the new motor age in contributing to the character of the contemporary decades, is worthy of special emphasis by social scientists. Even as early as 1910, when the total passenger car registration was some 458,000, many observers of American society were already commenting upon the potential social and economic impact of the new form of transportation. Each succeeding year brought an increase in registration figures. In 1915 some 2,332,000 automobiles were on American highways. In 1920 the figure was 8,131,000. At the close of the decade the passenger registration was 23,060,110. Even the low-point depression years of the 1930's brought only a slight decrease in the total automobile registration. In 1937 the total automobile registration was 27,372,000.

This staggering increase in registration suggests the rapid expansion of the manufacturing facilities of the automobile industry. Successful companies constructed new and large factories. The automotive industry, which introduced modern mass production techniques, continued to find new uses for machinery in production. The industry also further developed its successful distribution system through dealerships. Undoubtedly credit sales to purchasers also enlarged the annual market.

The automotive industry emphasized innovations to make the automobile safer, faster, and more comfortable. Millions of dollars were spent in research to achieve such breakthroughs as clear, unbreakable safety glass and sturdy brakes to accompany an age of speed. During the 1920's, the closed car, originally regarded as a luxury model, became the standard form. In 1925, for the first time, the sale of closed cars exceeded the sales of the open models.

The universal use of the automobile altered our social mores rapidly. On March 4, 1921, Warren G. Harding became the first president of our land to ride to his inauguration in an automobile. Earlier rural prejudice against the automobile also disappeared rapidly. In 1920 only 30.7 percent of the farms reported automobile ownership, while in 1930 the figure was 58.0 percent. During the same period truck ownership increased from 2.0 percent to 13.4 percent. The bus supplemented and sometimes replaced the streetcar and interurban railroad.

In spite of the increased production, fewer and fewer companies survived. Many companies could not secure adequate financing during the periods required to adjust to new marketing conditions and to the numerous technological changes. By the late 1920's Ford, General Motors, and Chrysler had become the "Big Three." General Motors was the brain child of W. C. Durant of Flint, Michigan, who was in all probability the first of the automotive pioneers to recognize the importance of large-scale reorganization as a requisite for success in the industry. In 1908 Durant formed General Motors Corporation, which acquired both the Olds and Buick plants. To the disappointment of Durant, Ford was unwilling to sell his interests to General Motors. In 1911, however, the Cadillac and Oakland (now the Pontiac) were acquired by General Motors. In 1918 Chevrolet became an integral part of General Motors.

The Chrysler Corporation was developed by Walter P. Chrysler, who received his automotive training with General Motors. In 1922 Chrysler reorganized the Maxwell and Chalmers companies, both of which were facing financial difficulties. In 1928 the Chrysler Corporation formally established in 1925, acquired the Dodge Motor Company, founded in 1914 by John and Horace Dodge. As a result of the Dodge purchase, Chrysler acquired additional facilities for mass production. The combination of adequate capital, trained personnel, established agencies, and modern factory facilities enabled Chrysler to become a major automotive company.

By 1920 Detroit was the undisputed center of the automotive industry. Its factories supplied a large portion of the cars sold annually in a growing market. Automotive policy was shaped in Detroit. Approximately forty percent of the industrial workers in Detroit owed their livelihood to the industry.

Fortunately for Detroit it was the major center for Ford and Chrysler operations. Cadillac and important units of the General Motors Corporation were also located in the city. Throughout the 1920's, Hudson, Packard, Hupp, and Graham-Paige supplemented the "Big-Three" in the creation of the industrial image of the city.

Wages in the automotive industry were higher in comparison with other industries, in spite of the few weeks of unemployment each year. Early in 1919 Henry Ford announced his six dollars a day minimum wage. The Ford bombshell affected all industries. The average daily wage in Detroit rose from $5.30 in 1919 to $6.20 in 1920.

A large number of Detroit laborers enjoyed two forms of ownership not shared by all American workers. The first, understandably, was the automobile. Detroit workers were among the first to drive to work. The second, home ownership, was further proof of a high standard of living. In 1919 approximately 13,000 new housing units were constructed. Some 7,100 units of this total were single residences.

The Detroit wage scale for the unskilled and semiskilled was, of course, highly publicized throughout the nation. Other aspects of the great automotive prosperity were also spectacular. The great increase in population and the rapid economic expansion resulted in a realty boom that brought wealth to many. The new tempo in construction brought additional fortunes. Early in 1900's it was not unusual for an individual to supervise the construction of his new home. Even professional builders did not undertake large-scale residential operations. In the 1920's realty subdividing be-

came highly specialized, calling for large capital requirements. Builders developed models for the construction of
single-residence homes on a mass basis.

Only a handful of wealthy Detroiters invested in the
pioneer automotive ventures. For many years Olds was the
only automobile stock listed on the Detroit Stock Exchange.
Gradually, however, Detroit citizens of means began to
purchase automotive shares. They sensed, quite correctly,
the future financial strength of the industry. Many, apparently, also welcomed the opportunity to invest in a local
industry. This desire to advance the economic future of the
"home town" appealed to many.

During this era of the boom 1920's, Detroit attracted national attention for reasons other than its industry. It became the center for the distribution of illicit liquor. In
1916 the Michigan electorate approved state prohibition.
The amendment became effective in 1918. Almost immediately a considerable amount of liquor was transported into
Detroit illegally from Canada and continued to be shipped
in increasingly large amounts after the entire nation had
become dry.

By 1921 huge amounts of illicit liquor were smuggled
across the Detroit River, with equal amounts being illegally
manufactured in the city. As a result of prohibition and the
traffic in liquor, Detroit became a great distribution center
for bootleggers. Gangs were organized to control the irregular trade, with "wars" taking place between the rival
groups. Organized crime and gang warfare remained until
the repeal of prohibition.

Almost immediately after the end of World War I the
skyline of Detroit received a major face-lifting. Included
in the huge building program of the 1920's were skyscrapers
that attracted the attention of architects throughout the
nation. The Penobscot Building, the tallest, highlighted the
downtown area. The Book brothers took the leadership in

transforming Washington Boulevard into a modern replica of New York's Fifth Avenue. The Book-Cadillac Hotel, located at Michigan and Washington, was the showplace of this new development.

In 1919 the General Motors Corporation began its construction of the largest office building in the Middle West. This marked the beginning of the "G. M. Area," centering around Second and East Grand Boulevard. In 1928 the Fisher Building won architectural recognition. In many respects the "G. M. Area" became Detroit's second "downtown."

The Detroit River was also the scene of great building activity. In 1928 the completion of the Detroit-Windsor Tunnel assured facilities for motorists who found the older ferry service to be totally inadequate. In 1929 the Ambassador Bridge was completed. This second link between Detroit and Windsor was as spectacular an engineering feat as had been the building of the tunnel.

In 1929 industry in Detroit was at a new peak, with the employment of approximately 330,000 men. Although the automotive industry indisputably ranked first, many other industries were far from insignificant. Pharmaceuticals, tobacco, copper, steel, printing, meat packing, and even industries making leisure-time goods contributed to the phenomenal economic tempo.

The Great Depression came to Detroiters with great suddenness, following an era of almost abnormal prosperity. The automotive and its related industries had been maintaining the high-wage scale. Many workers, in fact, were using their savings to enter other fields. The building trades were enjoying an unusual boom because of the need for construction of residences, business centers, new factories, and schools.

In retrospect many could point to danger signs. Apartment construction began to decline in 1926. Model changes

in the automotive plants sometimes resulted in lengthy intervals of unemployment. Several of the weaker independents in the automotive industry drastically reduced the
number of employees. Never, however, was there any real
basis for pessimism until the autumn of 1929.

The panic was unusually severe in Detroit. Unemployment and other warnings of a financial crisis could be observed as early as the summer of 1929. In 1930 the Depression was accompanied by layoffs, drastic reductions in
the working week, and an abnormal deflation. By mid-1931
mass unemployment had ruined thousands of people. All
segments of society in Detroit suffered from this economic
decline.

The increase in welfare costs, assumed by the city government, rose astronomically. In 1929 city officials assumed
that the relief load would not exceed 3,500 families. In
January of 1930 approximately 12,500 families received assistance. By the end of 1931 the figure had increased almost tenfold. The problem of welfare gave a new significance to Detroit's municipal government.

In a sense, the psychological impact of the new charter
upon the electorate was disappointing to the proponents of
reform. The achievements of the municipal government
simply did not arouse any great enthusiam. Although there
was little advance in long-term planning, the immediate
needs of the city were met, sometimes speedily so. City
services were extended to the outlying areas. Schools
and other essential services were made available. The extension of services during a period of rapid growth reduced
complaints against the municipal government to a minimum.

Unfortunately, municipal achievements could not easily
be communicated to the individual voter. The non-partisan
government ended the importance of the ward. Only the
ward organization could make municipal elections truly
exciting. Candidates, of course, discussed streetcar services,

the gang wars, and taxes. In effect, election issues were often reduced to a personal basis and whispering campaigns since there were so few real issues at stake.

The new charter had increased the power of the mayor. With the exception of James Couzens, the men who served as mayor throughout the 1920's failed to offer the leadership that the champions of the charter had anticipated. John C. Lodge was known to Detroiters as a faithful and conscientious councilman. John Smith became well known to the community as postmaster of Detroit. Frank Doremus had an excellent record as a member of Congress. All of the successful candidates had the endorsement of civic organizations. In the final analysis, however, the victor won a personality contest.

Although the new charter ended ward representation, the Council was representative of classes and religions. The men elected to the Council ordinarily had the endorsement of the Citizens' League. Many had been identified with civic organizations.

The uneventful character of city politics did not disappoint Detroiters who recalled the ills under the previous charter. The majority supported the new non-partisan government. The older generation, in particular, believed that the administration, under the new charter, had done a conscientious and creditable job.

In 1929 the interval of uneventful city politics ended with the election of Charles Bowles as mayor. His victory was a surprise. Bowles had been attacked in unsubstantiated whispering campaigns. Some charged that he had Klan endorsement; others warned that he would use his power to develop a "Republican machine" that would destroy the non-partisan character of Detroit government.

Bowles could not carry out his campaign pledge of economy because of the welfare burden. The majority of his recommendations aroused intense opposition. On July 22,

1930, less than seven months after his inauguration, Mayor Bowles was recalled by Detroiters at a special election.

His successor was Frank Murphy, a former municipal judge, whose political star was to rise very rapidly. He was Detroit's outstanding Democratic leader during the decade of the 1930's, and he became mayor at a time when the Great Depression was creating almost unsolvable problems for the city. Frank Murphy's program attracted national attention. In 1933, President Roosevelt appointed him to the office of Governor General of the Philippines. In 1936 he sought the office of Governor of Michigan and was elected. He subsequently served as Attorney General of the United States and then later was appointed a Justice of the United States Supreme Court.

Mayor Murphy was under heavy pressure. The very high rate of tax delinquency forced the city to borrow to meet immediate expenses. This, in turn, added to the debt service. Even in 1929 approximately twenty percent of the budget was allocated for debt service. By 1932 approximately forty percent was required for debt service. Welfare costs, of course, mounted as the Depression became more severe in Detroit.

The mayor adopted a middle-of-the-pond policy in the heated controversies between the welfare champions and the proponents of rigid economy. He ordered the public welfare officials to meet the steadily rising relief needs of the unemployed. At the same time he maintained the financial integrity of the municipal government.

Frank Murphy was one of the few mayors of his era to attract national attention. His bold program occasioned feelings that did not easily subside. The policies that he pursued to alleviate the immediate plight of the unemployed contributed to his future political popularity.

The Depression reached its most devastating point during the early weeks of 1933, when approximately one-third of the labor force was unemployed. A majority of these unfortunate men and women were dependent upon the municipal government for assistance. Several Detroit banks had failed before the state banking holiday was proclaimed in February of 1933. The decision of the Treasury not to allow two of the leading banks to reopen, after the nationwide decree had closed all banks, further injured the economy of the city. Strict economy budgets reduced the municipal services.

The New Deal relief policies relieved the city of a large portion of its public assistance program. Yet, throughout the 1930's the welfare load placed a financial burden upon the municipal government, since even the improvement in employment did not end the welfare problem. The welfare load, of course, tended to vary with automobile production. Even in December 1937, however, some thirteen percent of Detroit families were on relief.

Projects undertaken by the municipal government ordinarily were partially financed by federal aid. Criticism was often directed against city officials for failure to plan more definitely for a growing city of the future. Plans for rapid transit, including a subway network, did not advance beyond the discussion stages.

After 1933, a labor movement long dormant, came to life in Detroit. Between 1900 and 1910 Detroit labor seemed to lack the vitality of an era that had given birth to the Detroit Council of Trades. Although individual unions were active and frequently increased membership rolls, there was an absence of unity. Organized labor, however, was not a part of any major national mainstream. In fact, Detroit, in the opinion of many labor leaders, was a "poor union town."

The unusual growth of the city between 1910 and 1920 resulted in a large increase in membership of many craft unions, including the building trades. The Detroit Federa-

tion of Labor, successor to the Detroit Council, assumed a
new leadership. Organized labor became directly concerned with legislation at the national, state, and city
levels. To a very large extent labor gave its enthusiastic
support to progressivism. In particular, labor endorsed progressivism at the municipal level. In 1918 the Detroit Federation advocated municipal ownership of city utilities, an
eight-hour day for municipal employees, the creation of a
city department of labor to assure enforcement of factory
laws, an extension of park services, the immediate construction of more schools, an extension of the city market system, and a reduction of taxes on workingmen's homes.

The boom 1920's further strengthened the older and
highly specialized craft unions. The great majority of Detroit factory workers, however, were unorganized. In 1903
the Detroit Council had made feeble efforts to organize automotive workers. Other unsuccessful efforts were made in
1910 and in 1916. By 1920 many craft union leaders had,
apparently, become indifferent to the organization of automotive workers. Unions made little headway for several reasons. The automotive industry paid wages that were com-
paratively high, and opportunity for advancement was rapid.
A general lack of previous experience with labor organizations stayed the trend toward unionism. The industry employed many young men who hoped to enter other fields.
Thousands of the workers were from the rural regions. Another category of workers consisted of immigrants who had
not been affiliated with unions in the country of their birth.
Undoubtedly, the majority of automotive workers associated
job security with a growing industry.

The Great Depression had an immediate impact upon
automotive employees. The working week was drastically
reduced for those lucky enough to remain on the payroll. A
large number were without any employment for months.
Many of the married men had purchased homes during the

prosperous 1920's. Thus, the typical worker not only found himself unemployed, but faced the loss of his accumulated savings. The sudden lowering of the standard of living, previously taken for granted, created a general feeling of insecurity.

From the first, the New Deal undertook a comprehensive program to strengthen the position of labor. Undoubtedly, the legislation assuring the right of collective bargaining was labor's most valuable gain. New rights granted to labor by the National Industrial Recovery Act, and subsequently by the Wagner Act, did not, however, immediately give rise to a clear labor picture in Detroit. The older craft unions, affiliated with the American Federation of Labor, increased their membership as more men received employment in the trades. Often these unions were immediately able to negotiate new and favorable contracts.

The automotive workers, however, had no immediate background of unionism. In the early months of the New Deal, the American Federation and the Industrial Workers of the World (I.W.W.) made ineffective overtures to the automobile workers. In fact, the inroads of the I.W.W. were entirely negligible. Several independent unions made their appearances, and a brief period of labor instability followed.

In 1935 leading proponents of industrialism within the American Federation of Labor formed the Committee on Industrial Organization (C.I.O.). In the following year the Executive Council of the A.F.L. suspended the unions represented in this body. Included among the C.I.O. unions was the United Automobile Workers (U.A.W.), a union which stressed the organization of all grades of automobile workers on an industrial basis.

The C.I.O. victories in the automotive industry were achieved by the introduction of a new technique, the sit-down strike, whereby workers took possession of a plant and refused to allow company officials to enter. In 1936 this technique was successfully employed against the General Motors at Flint. As a result, the U.A.W. was recognized as the bargaining agent for employees of General Motors.

The U.A.W. then engineered a sit-down strike of the workers of the Chrysler Corporation and won recognition as the bargaining agency with that corporation. The growing automotive union failed, however, in its initial attempts to unionize the giant Ford Motor Company. Not until 1941, when defense work was so essential, did Ford accept the U.A.W. as the bargaining agent for its many thousands of employees.

The U.A.W. has been an aggressive organization, and its leadership has been recruited, in part, from Detroit members. Walter Reuther attained national prominence as a labor leader. In fact, his reputation has transcended the field of labor. The U.A.W. did not confine its demands merely to issues of wage increases. It also made requests for welfare programs and a partial determination of the rate of production. In fact, the U.A.W. contracts have been highly influential in establishing precedents for negotiations by other unions.

The C.I.O. actively entered into political contests. The vast majority of the local C.I.O. endorsements went to Democrats, thereby strengthening the party. The Democratic Party lost heavily during the 1920's. The first significant gains were made in the general election of 1930. By 1933 Wayne County had become a Democratic stronghold. The C.I.O. endeavored to consolidate these new gains. More significantly, it attempted to assure a strong labor leadership within the Democratic Party.

Strangely enough, labor did not show unusual strength in the Detroit non-partisan elections. Labor-endorsed candidates for mayor were defeated on a number of occasions, and labor-supported candidates for the City Council likewise had only nominal success.

A degree of labor unrest could, however, be observed in Detroit even during intervals of apparent calm. A city, previously unaccustomed to aggressive unionism, became a virtual headquarters for a new labor pattern.

Throughout the Depression so-called psychological factors were important in determining Detroit's mood. In contrast with the 1920's its residents appeared to lack enthusiasm. Deflation had destroyed vast sums. Many Detroiters had lost confidence and were leary of the future of their city. Indices of moderate recovery did not resemble the huge gains of the preceding decade. In 1926 Detroit building permits totaled 40,200 for a value of $183,000,000. In 1933 the 4,070 permits had a total value of $3,945,000. In 1937 the 16,400 permits had a value of $52,000,000. Although Detroiters were gratified in 1937 at the increase over 1933, many thought with nostalgia of 1926.

Although many Detroiters lost confidence in the future of their city during the Depression, even a casual appraisal at the outbreak of World War II was indicative of a pride in past accomplishments and great hopes of the people for the future. Detroit was a great industrial complex. The 2,700 industrial establishments in the area gave employment to 311,000. The automotive industry, of course, ranked first. The iron and steel, leather, chemical, and machinery (excluding electrical) industries followed in order of their importance.

After the outbreak of World War II in 1939, many Detroit citizens, of course, engaged in the spirited discussion about foreign policy. By the autumn of 1941, the average Detroiter was uncertain of the prospects of actual involvement in a shooting war. Many believed that aid, short of war, given to the Allies would lead to the defeat of the aggressor nations. Others desired American participation as the means of assuring the defeat.

The attack on Pearl Harbor ended all speculation. Detroit, like every other American community, large and small, was part of an all-out action of total war. Both the length of World War II and the scale in which it was fought called for tremendous efforts. A steady flow of men and women left the city to serve in the armed forces in the greatest human mobilization that our nation has known.

Detroit began to feel the economic impact of the war as early as the summer of 1940 when the inauguration of a defense plan marked the beginnings of a new phase of industrial growth. After Pearl Harbor the goals of war production were staggering. Early in the war, Detroit production engineers took their first steps for the rapid conversion of plants from civilian products to war materials. For example, they ended all civilian automobile production. The automobile factories produced a number of war items. The industry made an impressive record for its production of airplanes and airplane engines, tanks, and anti-aircraft guns. Both small and large establishments were converted to war production.

This step was essential, since the construction of the many new factories authorized often required months. Immediately upon completion, however, these new plants engaged in war production. Typical of these new large factories was the immediately famous Willow Run Bomber Plant near Ypsilanti, operated by the Ford Motor Company. At its peak period of production, this giant plant employed 42,000 workers. This one plant alone built over 8,600 of the very effective B-24 Liberator bombers. The huge tank arsenal operated by the Chrysler Corporation produced 25,000 tanks.

Detroit deservedly became known as the "Arsenal of Democracy." The entire industrial potential of the metropolitan area was strained in efforts toward greater production for war. Detroit production engineers overcame mountains of obstacles—obstacles psychological as well as material—to effect the tremendous production schedules.

Large numbers of men in the armed services were stationed in the Detroit area. Selfridge trained hundreds for aerial warfare. The Grosse Ile Naval Base also trained many aviators. Large military airports were located at Romulus and Willow Run. The Dearborn Naval School, in cooperation with the Ford Motor Company, gave highly technical instruction to hundreds of mechanics.

Popular participation in a number of home-front programs contributed to the war effort in Detroit. Unlike World War I, the American people were encouraged to buy bonds regularly instead of waiting for drives. Many purchased bonds on a payroll deduction plan. Many Detroit men and women, however, were active in several supplementary drives conducted to intensify bond sales. Campaigns for the Red Cross and for the several relief organizations exceeded their quotas. U.S.O. centers offered recreational facilities for thousands of service men and women.

A highly efficient civilian-defense program gave technical training to 110,000 Detroit men and women. In this impressive total were 55,000 air-raid workers, 13,000 medical service volunteers, and 7,500 auxiliary firemen. The leaders of the civilian defense projects were universally successful in their program of alerting citizens to potential dangers.

Detroit experienced real growing pains. Its huge labor force was recruited not from newcomers alone but also from large numbers of women, single and married. Housing shortages and overcrowding helped to create racial tensions. The serious social dislocation in Detroit was most painfully observed in the race riot of June, 1943, when thirty-five individuals (including twenty-eight Negroes) were killed, approximately 1,000 persons injured, and some $2,-000,000 worth of property destroyed in looting and rioting. Detroit's early Negro population of a few hundred increased to 12,000 in the half century between 1860 and 1910. During World War I many Negroes were encouraged to migrate to Detroit. In 1917 several Detroit companies advertised in cities of the South for Negro labor. The Negro population jumped to 40,000 between 1910 and 1920, and stood at 100,-000 twenty years later. It was estimated that the city had a Negro population of well over 152,000 in 1943. Housing congestion, discrimination, and a lack of adequate social and recreational facilities for the Negroes were accompanied by numerous tensions that culminated in the June disaster. Fortunately, leaders of both races immediately labored to restore amity and to improve social conditions.

The occurrence of the race riots should not suggest that Detroit was a city with major social scars. In fact, throughout the entire interval between 1900 and 1945, Detroit accommodated itself to major changes with a minimum of friction. Detroit's rapid growth attracted the immigrant. In 1910 the foreign-born comprised 156,000 of the total population of 465,000. The foreign-born included 44,000 Germans, 41,000 Canadians, 18,000 Russians, 14,000 Austrians, and 9,200 English. Other nationalities were also well represented, since the foreign-born included 5,900 Hungarians, 5,700 Italians, 5,500 Irish, 3,300 Scottish, and 3,200 Belgians.

Prosperity brought newcomers from all areas. Many of Detroit's new residents were from states other than Michigan. In 1910 approximately 6,000 Detroiters were from New York State; 3,400 from Ohio; and 1,200 from Pennsylvania. Detroit had not drawn large numbers of Midwesterners, other than from Ohio. In 1920 the foreign-born comprised 29.1 percent of the total population. The 289,200 foreign-born included 58,500 Canadians, 56,600 Polish, 30,000 Germans, 27,200 Russians, 17,100 English, 16,000 Italians, 13,-500 Hungarians, 10,700 Austrians, 7,000 Irish, and 6,900 Scottish. The immigrants in Detroit tended to reflect, in part, the national pattern. The large number of Canadians can be explained by the city's proximity to the border.

A large portion of the labor force required during the 1920's was supplied by men and women who moved to Detroit from other parts of the United States. Many were unemployed miners from Michigan's Upper Peninsula. Others came from the fast disappearing lumbering areas. The larger numbers, however, came from the farms. The Negro migration to Detroit was significant. In 1930 a total of 74.1 percent of the total population was native-born.

The 94,200 Canadians comprised the largest group among the foreign-born. The 66,100 Polish, 32,700 Germans, 28,600 English, 28,500 Italians, 23,500 Scottish, 21,700 Russians, and 11,100 Hungarians indicate the diversity of Detroit's foreign-born.

A mature Detroit accepted the increased heterogeneity of the city. The many ethnic groups added to the cosmopolitan character of Detroit's economic and social life. Men of foreign birth or foreign background were well represented in the commercial and political life of the city.

The physical growth of Detroit increased the problems of the municipal government. In 1857 Detroit had an area of twelve square miles. In 1918 the city acquired twenty-one square miles by annexation. This expansion, of course, played a role in securing the adoption of a new charter.

The problem of serving outlying areas remained acute throughout the 1920's. By 1927 Detroit had an area of 139 square miles. The mounting cost of enlarging the municipal services to outlying districts resulted in an opposition to further annexations.

Yet, the Detroit municipal government was well aware of the problems resulting from the fantastic growth. Through out the decade of the 1920's in particular, governmental services were rapidly expanded to keep pace with the population growth. During a very critical period Frank Cody,

Superintendent of Schools, made every effort to assure adequate facilities and to recruit a competent staff. A network of new neighborhood libraries supplemented the services of the new main library.

The achievements of the Department of Health received national commendation. The three municipal hospitals—Receiving, Herman Keifer, and Maybury—supplemented the growing list of privately supported hospitals. The Department of Health sponsored programs of care and of education. Through its efforts the death rate from contagious diseases was drastically reduced.

The city government was liberal in its appropriations for public parks; all of them drew large crowds. In 1913 attendance was 1,790,000, and by 1928 the figure was 12,000,000.

The utilities also made a frequently overlooked contribution to Detroit, each one enlarging its budget for construction. The municipally owned water works and the privately owned gas, electric, and phone companies made their services available to the many new neighborhoods. The increase in residential phone service after 1916 was staggering.

By 1916 the phenomenal increase in wealth gave Detroit an air of cosmopolitan and sophistication previously lacking. Nightclubs within the city limits were numerous, with exclusive roadhouses on the outskirts. Three residential areas for families of means could be recognized. The Indian Village and North Woodward neighborhoods were within the city limits. The expanding Grosse Pointe was among Detroit's few residential suburbs. Middle-class neighborhoods were numerous.

People of means identified themselves closely with their city. The new wealth helped to support the theater and expensive dining places. The growth of the city and the increase in wealth encouraged the expansion of social clubs, which soon became an accepted characteristic of Detroit's community life. Many of the new organizations promoted civic efforts and helped to create a social consciousness.

Detroit's cultural life did not lag. Formal art organizations continued to promote interest in the fine arts. The Detroit Society of Women Painters was organized in 1903 and immediately became active in conducting exhibits. The Scarab Club of Detroit is another important organization of artists which has been unusually successful in recent decades. It includes among its members many of the leading men and women practicing the arts in the Detroit area. The fine arts were among the few fields that received new sources of support during the Depression of the 1930's. The Works Project Administration (W.P.A.) employed a large number of persons in the allied fields of painting, sculpture, literature, and the drama.

Detroit was the home of many artists of distinction. Julius Theodore Melchers, a sculptor and woodcarver of considerable reputation, lived in Detroit from 1855 until his death in 1903. He inspired and taught others in architecture and the fine arts. He was the father of Gari Melchers, whose murals adorn the present Detroit Public Library.

Detroit-born Julius Rolshoven received his training in New York and in Europe. Although much of his painting was done in Italy, he frequently returned to the city of his birth for long periods.

Percy Ives, son of the distinguished portrait artist Lewis T. Ives, was born in Detroit in 1864. He followed in his father's footsteps as a portrait painter. His reputation was assured at an early age. He was invited to paint the portraits of President Cleveland and other distinguished Americans. Ives followed the profession of portrait painting in Detroit until his death in 1928.

The Detroit Symphony Orchestra, organized in 1872, remained active until 1910. After that date the Detroit Orchestral Society sponsored concerts by symphony orchestras from other cities. Interest in these programs led to the revival of the Detroit Symphony Orchestra, which in 1919 secured the services of Ossip Gabrilowitch as its director. This orchestra was liberally and enthusiastically supported and, under Gabrilowitch and other outstanding directors, became one of the best-known orchestras in the nation. It reached large audiences through concert tours. The Detroit Civic Operetta Company was organized in 1928 by Thaddeus Wronski, who served both as general manager and director of the chorus and stage.

Many bands have played to receptive and enthusiastic audiences in Detroit. Before World War I various itinerant bands, known as German bands because a portion of the personnel was of German origin, played on street corners merely for donations from listeners. After World War I, the city government sponsored frequent concerts at Belle Isle.

By the 1920's motion pictures had become a major pastime. Early in the century they were considered as little more than a novelty. A brief "movie" was often shown as a minor feature at the Temple or other vaudeville houses. By 1916, however, a host of stars, including Mary Pickford and Charlie Chaplin, had become box-office attractions. Within three years first-run theaters were featuring massive productions.

The "movie house" was as conscious of its patrons as were the producers. The leading theaters incorporated all of the comforts of the earlier opera house, and the largest among them employed orchestras to accompany silent films. Even after the introduction of sound movies, orchestras supplemented the main features.

The Capitol, the Fox, and the Broadway were among the leading downtown movie houses. Large neighborhood houses were also constructed. In 1928 the new Fisher movie theater occupied a portion of the magnificent Fisher Building. The success of the motion picture industry indicated that Detroiters, like all Americans, were using a larger portion of their leisure for commercial recreation.

Commercial sports increased in popularity. Even before World War I the Detroit Tigers had an unusually large following. The feats of Tyrus (Ty) Raymond Cobb, a skilled outfielder, gave the Tigers distinction. Loyal fans, however, were disappointed with the standing of the Tigers, who had won their last pennant in 1908 under the leadership of Hugh Jennings. Not until 1934, in the post-Cobb era, did the Tigers win another pennant, under the new catcher-manager Mickey Cochrane. In the following year they won the baseball championship by defeating the St. Louis Cardinals.

Hockey teams played before large crowds at the 17,000 seat Olympia which was constructed in 1928. Here the Red Wings brought Detroit its first Stanley Cup in 1935. Professional football made a slow start. Many enthusiasts continued to follow high school and collegiate teams. By 1935 the championship Detroit Lions had demonstrated their abilities to growing crowds.

Native-born Joe Louis added to the stature of fighting by his successful quest for the heavyweight championship in 1937. Other Detroiters made substantial success in prize fighting. Fight promoters found large audiences among Detroit fans.

Not all sport enthusiasts preferred the spectacular. Golf, earlier regarded as a hobby for the very wealthy, became practically a national game after World War I. During the 1920's and 1930's many courses, public and private, were developed in the Detroit area to accommodate the enthusiasts.

CHAPTER V

The Metropolitan Area (1946-Present)

After World War II, Detroiters gradually came to recognize the importance of the metropolitan area. This term was formally recognized by the Census Bureau in 1930. Technically the metropolitan area consists of a major city, known as the core or inner city, and the communities that have grown up beyond its city limits. These satellite communities are, of course, identified with the inner city. All are a part of a metropolitan economy and a metropolitan culture. Ideally, all of these many political entities should cooperate in solving the many problems of modern urbanization. In practice, however, the metropolitan concept cannot be implemented in a day. Governmental rivalries must be overcome and legal barriers surmounted.

The Detroit metropolitan area is primarily composed of the three counties of Wayne, Oakland, and Macomb. It includes, in addition, small portions of Washtenaw and Monroe counties. Undoubtedly, other areas will be added in the near future.

In 1950 the area had a population of 3,016,000. Detroit, with its 1,845,000 inhabitants, was larger by far than the outlying communities, with a total population of 1,166,000. In 1960 the Detroit area ranked fifth in the nation with a population of 3,762,000. The city proper had a population of 1,670,000, representing a decline of almost ten percent. The outlying communities had a total population of 2,092,000 and registered a gain of approximately eighty percent. The entire metropolitan area population was increased by twenty-five percent. Only the Los Angeles-Long Beach area could show a higher rate of increase.

The increase, for example, for Chicago, was only twenty percent.

The increase in population in Oakland and Macomb counties was astronomical. Between 1950 and 1960 the former increased from 396,000 to 690,000 by a ratio of approximately seventy-five percent. Macomb increased from 184,000 to 405,000, showing a gain of one hundred and twenty percent.

Some suburban cities virtually came into existence between 1950 and 1960. In 1950 Warren had a population of 727. Ten years later the figure was 89,246. Livonia's population jumped from 17,534 to 66,702. St. Clair Shores grew from 19,823 to 76,657. Some of the older suburbs also experienced an unusual expansion. The population of East Detroit increased from 25,461 to 45,756. During the same decade the population of Allen Park increased from 12,329 to 37,494.

Some of the older communities within the metropolitan area followed the Detroit pattern and registered a decline in population. In this category were Highland Park and Hamtramck. Highland Park also lost, in part, because of the declining importance of the Ford plant in the city.

The suburban communities were more than mere residential adjuncts. Industry also found its way to the outlying areas. This trend began with the construction of defense plants beyond town limits just before World War II. By 1960, however, several industrial zones had been created. One was located in Warren. Another large belt was found in the Wixom-Grand River area.

Suburban residents no longer found it necessary to shop in downtown Detroit. The J. L. Hudson Company introduced a new trend by making adequate retail facilities available with the construction of Northland. This center included an entire retail complex. The J. L. Hudson Company elaborated upon the new pattern with the construction of similar centers at convenient suburban locations. By 1960 many firms had founded their own centers.

The suburbs were never entirely self-contained. Their residents relied upon the inner city for many cultural activities. The Detroit newspapers found their way to the outlying areas. The *Detroit News,* which absorbed the *Times,* and the *Free Press,* provided adequate suburban coverage. The central city served further as the communication lifeline through the mediums of radio and television.

Differentials in education between Detroit and the suburbs are significant. In the metropolitan area 40.9 percent of the population had completed four years of high school or more. For Detroit the figure was 34.4 percent. On the other hand, in the suburbs 47.5 percent had completed four years of high school or more. In the metropolitan area the median school years completed was 10.8 years. In Detroit proper the median was 10.0 years and 11.7 years in the suburbs.

In 1960 the population of the metropolitan area remained very cosmopolitan. The foreign-born constituted 9.7 percent of the population. Some 20.4 percent were native-born of foreign or native-foreign parentage. Detroit's population, however, had definite Michigan moorings, inasmuch as 65.8 percent of the native population was born in the state.

Manufacturing industries gave employment to 40.7 percent of the population. The high percentage engaged in manufacturing continued to stamp Detroit as an industrial city. Over two out of five, however, were white-collar workers, with a total of 43.1 percent of Detroit residents in this category.

Discrepancies between the income of Detroiters living within the city and the income of suburban residents were significant. The median family income for the metropolitan area was $6,825. The median income for Detroit proper, however, was $6,069, in contrast with a median suburban income of $7,472. Although 13.5 percent of the families in the metropolitan area had an annual income of less than $3,000, the figure for Detroit was 19.0 percent; in the suburbs only 8.6 percent of the families had an income of less than $3,000. The suburbs also had a greater percentage with incomes over $10,000. In the metropolitan area 21.9 percent had incomes of $10,000 or more. In Detroit proper the figure was 17.8 percent. In the suburbs, however, 25.7 percent of the families reported an annual income of $10,000 or more.

Residents of the metropolitan area have had sufficient income to own their own homes. In 1960 the Detroit metropolitan area had 1,153,000 dwelling units. Approximately sixty percent were single residences and of these a very large majority were owned by the residents. Only eleven percent of the units were apartments.

Some aspects of recreation gave evidence of a metropolitan area even before the term was in common use. The new trend is well illustrated by parks. Detroit's early parks were ordinarily within the city limits and reached by inexpensive public transportation. Although Rouge Park was spacious and emphasized a new pattern of tennis courts and other recreational facilities, it was fundamentally a city park. By the middle 1950's Detroiters in larger numbers were finding their way to Kensington Park outside the city limits. Even more illustrative of the new trend was the creation of a separate governmental unit to supervise Metropolitan Beach.

Rapid changes in aviation called attention to the inadequacies of the jammed Detroit City Airport located on Gratiot Avenue. Detroiters, however, could not agree upon the location of an airport adequate to care for the larger and faster planes. Neighborhood associations fought the proposal to locate the field in Northwest Detroit. Plans for an international airport at Windsor met with countless objections. In the meanwhile, Willow Run became the major airport in the area. Wayne County also enlarged its airport. Gradually, major carriers began to use its facilities. Finally, Metropolitan or "Metro," as it is now known, came to be, for all practical purposes, the area airport. This development illustrates a role of the county government in the evolution of a metropolitan area.

The parent city was the original focal point in expressway construction. As a new metropolitan pattern was developed, some of the arteries did not even "touch upon" the central city. The major plans were developed by the State Highway Department.

Automotive transportation was facilitated by the construction of expressways. Although the Detroit area had, at an early date, assumed a leadership in advanced forms of highway construction, it was slow to inaugurate a system of express highways. The Willow Run Expressway was partially constructed during World War II. After the war this expressway was extended as an east-west highway and named in honor of Edsel Ford. The city also undertook the construction of the north-south John Lodge Expressway. In the 1960's, an East Side–North-South highway, the Walter Chrysler Expressway, was constructed. These expressways, supplemented by a host of others, reduced travel time between the inner city and the outlying communities.

In 1960 there was a daily influx of some 231,000 suburbanites to Detroit. Public transportation plays an insignificant role in bringing this number to Detroit. Automotive ownership is high, and the representative suburban dweller travels a considerable distance on highways that permit speedy transportation.

Although Detroit and the suburbs are linked by many systems of public transportation, only one railroad, the

Grand Trunk, offers regular commuter service. This line enables North Woodward residents to travel between downtown Detroit and Pontiac by rail.

Two Detroit municipal services have been made available to many of the suburbs. The D.S.R. was extended into several of the suburbs to afford an inexpensive mode of public transportation to Detroit. Also, the city of Detroit entered into contracts to supply many of the suburbs with water.

The metropolitan area contributed to a common United Fund for charities. This Fund was the outgrowth of an earlier Community Fund Drive which represented a departure from an era when individual agencies vied for funds. The United Capital Fund Drive sponsored long-term projects such as hospitals.

In many respects the metropolitan culture overshadows other aspects of the metropolitan concept. The new metropolitan culture marks a real cultural renaissance. Apparently Detroit has accepted the belief that cultural facilities bring culture to a community. The idea of mass culture has brought about opposition in some areas. Detroit has given an affirmative answer to this much debated question.

Wayne State University represents the growth of democratic civic life in Detroit. Wayne State University stands as an expression of the enlargement of democatic civic consciousness in Detroit. Wayne is the outgrowth of the merger of several separate colleges maintained by the Detroit Board of Education. Although the university did not come into official existence until 1933—the name Wayne being given to it the following year—some of its colleges had already enjoyed a lengthy history. The history of its medical college can be traced to 1868; its college of education is the successor to the teacher training school established by the city in 1881. The liberal arts college is the outgrowth of post-graduate high school training offered at the Detroit Central High School in 1915. The popularity of this program led to the establishment of the junior college in 1917. Six years later, with state authorization, the junior college became a four-year collegiate degree–granting institution. The need for greater integration among these various city-operated colleges brought about the organization of the university, which now includes several professional schools in addition to those already mentioned. In 1958 the school came under state control and support and received its present name of Wayne State University.

The University of Detroit was founded in 1877 by the Jesuits. Its two campuses serve thousands of students. In addition to a college of liberal arts and the graduate school the University of Detroit operates several professional schools including a college of commerce and finance, a college of engineering and architecture, a law school, and a school of dentistry. Several liberal arts colleges for women are operated by Roman Catholic orders. These include Marygrove, originally located at Monroe, Michigan, Mercy, and Madonna colleges.

The Detroit Institute of Technology maintains a liberal arts college and professional schools. The school is an outgrowth of schools founded by the Y.M.C.A. The Lawrence Institute of Technology offers instruction primarily in architecture, engineering, and industrial management.

Two of the city's universities are post-World War II in origin. The campus of the Dearborn Center of the University of Michigan occupies a portion of "Fair Lane," the estate of the late Henry Ford. The Dearborn Center offers instruction primarily to college seniors and graduate students. Oakland University, in the Rochester-Pontiac area, opened its doors in 1959. It was originally affiliated with Michigan State University.

The Merrill-Palmer School began instruction in 1922. The school was established with funds left by Lizzie Pitts Merrill Palmer, the widow of the former Senator Thomas Palmer. The institution offers programs with an emphasis upon human development and the family.

The Detroit area supports many junior colleges. The pioneer was Highland Park Junior College which was founded in 1919. Henry Ford Community College and the South Macomb Junior College had large enrollments in the early 1960's.

The development of a contemporary interest in local history further indicates the appearance of a new type of civic pride. In 1921 a mere handful formed the Detroit Historical Society. In 1928 quarters were obtained in the Barlum Tower for a museum. In 1943 the initial plans for a museum building took form. Before the close of World War II, the building fund had been assured. The society, however, agreed to transfer the funds and other assets to the city in return for a pledge of municipal construction and maintenance of a museum. The electorate approved of the proposal. In 1950 construction of a museum began at Woodward and Kirby, its location making it a part of the cultural center. In 1951 the museum was opened as a part of the 250th anniversary. Since that time this museum at Woodward and Kirby has been supplemented by a military museum at Fort Wayne and a marine museum on Belle Isle.

Municipal appropriations for educational and library facilities have been adequate. The city government operates the Detroit Institute of Arts. The municipal government at an early date sponsored band concerts. Organizations and individuals have likewise generously supplemented the municipal government in sponsoring concerts open to the public, affording thousands an opportunity to enjoy good music during the summer months.

The cultural renaissance gave promise of a revived interest in the theater. Until 1930 Detroit had been known as a "good show town." The many legitimate theaters drew large and enthusiastic audiences. Much credit for the interest in drama should be given to Jessie Bonstelle, managing director of the Bonstelle Players. For many years the Bonstelle Players, formed by Miss Bonstelle in 1910, had almost the character of a civic theater. Miss Bonstelle trained a large number of future Broadway and movie stars. After 1925 the group had its own theater, the Bonstelle Playhouse, in the reconverted Temple Beth El on Woodward Avenue.

During the 1930's, the Depression and competition from the cinema brought dark days to the theater in Detroit. The Bonstelle and several houses failed to survive. The W.P.A. dramatic projects had only a minor impact upon the stage in Detroit.

The post-World War II prosperity, of course, improved the prospects for the theaters. Considerable credit should be given to the University Theater of Wayne State University and other experimental groups for rekindling a new enthusiasm for drama. In 1963 the Fisher Theater, reconverted from a motion-picture house, became Detroit's leading theater. The new Fisher policy was a most significant epoch in the revitalization of the legitimate theater in Detroit.

The Detroit area has two very unusual cultural attractions. Greenfield Village in Dearborn was developed by Henry Ford. Its authentic historical environment recreates the atmosphere of small-town life in the second half of the nineteenth century. The museum has a particular appeal for students of American technological history. The Cranbrook Foundation in Bloomfield Hills was founded by Ellen Scripps Booth and George G. Booth. The Foundation established the Cranbrook complex of schools, including the Cranbrook Academy of Art and the Cranbrook Institute of Science.

Several of Detroit's suburbs shared the phenomenal growth of the parent city. Highland Park was almost exclusively a product of the rapid rise of the Ford Motor Company. Although this community was incorporated as a village in 1889, its population remained almost stationary until 1909 when Henry Ford purchased a tract of one hundred and sixty acres as a site for the construction of a new major plant for the Ford Motor Company. Within one year the population of Highland Park increased from 425 to 4,120. In 1920 Highland Park had approximately 47,000 residents, attaining a peak population by 1930. The gradual abandonment of the Ford operations in the decades of the 1940's and 1950's was accompanied by a decline in population; by 1960 the number of residents had fallen to 38,000.

Dearborn became known in 1836 when the federal government chose it as a site for an arsenal. The village, named in honor of General Henry Dearborn, was for a short time called Dearbornville. In 1876 the arsenal was closed. The community continued, however, as a small commercial center. Modern Dearborn actually owes its importance to Henry Ford. This present-day home of the Ford Motor Company was also the birthplace of its founder. In 1893 Dearborn was incorporated as a village. For many years it remained a small distribution point, and as late as 1925, when Dearborn became a city, its population was not large.

In the interim, a small city called Springwells grew rapidly, with the location of the Rouge Plant of the Ford Motor Company within its limits. The government of Springwells changed the name of the community to Fordson, then Dearborn and Fordson were merged as the city of Dearborn.

Hamtramck became a major suburb because of the automotive industry. In 1901 it took form as a community when it assumed the status of a village. In 1910 the Dodge Brothers began the manufacture of automotive parts there.

In 1914 the famous automotive family began production of their own make of car in an enlarged plant. Hamtramck grew rapidly, but did not become a city until 1922. The community had a very large Polish population. Other ethnic groups, however, were well represented. Between 1930 and 1960 Hamtramck suffered a decline from 56,000 to 34,000 in population.

Grosse Pointe Shores, Grosse Pointe Farms, Grosse Pointe, and Grosse Pointe Park are separate governmental units that constitute the community of Grosse Pointe. This suburban community became a wealthy residential section even before the peak of the automotive industry. During the latter years of the nineteenth century, many Detroiters of means built summer homes in Grosse Pointe. By 1900 a large number lived there and used public transportation to reach downtown Detroit. By 1910 Grosse Pointe had acquired the character of a residential suburb.

The "down river" cities of River Rouge, Ecorse, and Wyandotte, even before 1900 constituted an industrial complex of communities similar to the Calumet area in Chicago. All of these cities were part of a separate industrial zone. By way of illustration, in 1864 a Wyandotte shop produced the first steel made in the United States by the Bessemer process. Wyandotte was also the home of thriving shipyards. In 1920 the combined population of the down-river cities, even before Detroit began to expand, was some 35,000. The area shared in the growth of Detroit's industrialism. Moreover, all were a part of greater Detroit because of railroad transportation, and, at a later date, interurban transportation.

The early Detroit satellites were not part of a planned suburban trend. The evolution was slow, with almost a complete absence of promotion. Many suburbs, planned as communities in the 1920's, had only a nominal growth until after 1945. After World War II Detroiters became more suburbia conscious. Although many suburban residents work in the suburbs in which they live or in other suburbs, because the metropolitan area network of highways makes this possible, still, in 1960 there was a daily influx of some 231,000 suburbanites into Detroit.

Many of Detroit's suburbs are primarily residential. Among the older suburbs, Huntington Woods and Royal Oak are primarily residential communities. Many of the recently developed suburbs have taken positive steps to retain a non-urban character. Franklin and West Bloomfield Township reflect this novel trend.

Detroit's residential suburbs have certain common characteristics. There is an unusual emphasis upon home ownership, with a surprisingly low percentage of apartment homes. Public transportation plays an insignificant role. Automotive ownership is high, and the representative suburban dweller travels a considerable distance on highways that permit speedy transportation.

Local government tends to be non-partisan. The commission-manager form of urban government is not uncommon. Royal Oak accepted this form of city administration at an early date. City planning has been an important aspect of government. Various civic organizations have promoted a community spirit. Schools and cultural projects have added to this consciousness. Community papers have been unusually important.

The Detroit municipal government was restricted in many of its programs because of inadequate revenues. The loss of industries, the decline in many property values, and the virtual absence of undeveloped land for industrial, commercial, and residential purposes combined to cripple the city in its search for more funds. State aid was earmarked and limited. The great strain placed upon the city because of welfare requirements called attention to its financial plight. Pension obligations and other fixed charges added to the cost of municipal government. Various proposals advanced to secure the needed funds met with opposition. Finally, in 1962, Detroit imposed a one-percent income tax to supplement the revenue secured from the more conventional sources of taxation.

The city government, however, was never stagnant. It implemented plans for the civic center, an area along the Detroit River from Randolph to Third and extending south of Jefferson. One of the units, the City-County Building, houses governmental offices. The other buildings, the Veterans Memorial Hall, the Ford Auditorium, and Cobo Hall serve general purposes.

The impressive Civic Center is located in an older area of the city. Its construction was, in part, incorporated in an urban redevelopment plan. The larger portion of Detroit's redevelopment program was given over to housing. The Lafayette was the first of these several programs. In 1962 Detroit began its redevelopment program for a new medical center. Initial steps were taken, also, to implement the long awaited international village program.

Wayne County also enlarged its services. The county government increased its appropriations for highways and welfare. Wayne County officials likewise pointed to the limitations of county income.

Every effort was made to call attention to Detroit's "growing pains." This growth, alone, made necessary greater expenditures by the city and county government. Both governmental units had to overcome some of the slacks of the Depression era.

Edward Jeffries, Jr., Eugene Van Antwerp, Albert Cobo, Louis Miriani, and Jerome Cavanagh served as mayors in the critical years since the end of World War II. All have been alert to modern urban problems. All attempted to adhere to Detroit's non-partisan philosophy of government.

The Common Council was not subject to drastic upheavals in personnel. The entire personnel in government gave its attention to the new urban problems. Only one of the mayors, Albert Cobo, sought promotion to state office. In 1956 he was nominated for governor on the Republican ticket, but was defeated by Governor G. Mennen Williams.

The pattern of Detroit's government has remained relatively undisturbed. Proposed charter amendments have not been numerous. The electorate ordinarily has approved amendments that would correct inequities or promote better government.

In partisan elections Detroit, as well as Wayne County, remains Democratic. Elsewhere in the metropolitan area the parties have shown almost equal strength. In 1960 in Detroit, John Swainson, a Democrat, polled 503,000 votes in the race for governor. His Republican opponent, Paul Bagwell, received 226,000 votes. In Wayne County the results were Swainson 790,000 and Bagwell 408,000. In Macomb County Swainson received 101,000 votes in comparison with 63,000 for Bagwell. On the other hand, in Oakland County Swainson led Bagwell by a margin of 164,000 to 130,000.

Labor's political role has been recognized by national leaders. Former President Truman began his vigorous 1948 campaign for reelection in Detroit on Labor Day. Adlai E. Stevenson also began his official 1952 and 1956 campaigns in Detroit on Labor Day. In 1960 President Kennedy began his campaign at the Labor Day parade. In 1964 President Johnson continued the tradition by launching his formal campaign in a Labor Day address at Cadillac Square.

Detroit's economy remains fundamentally automotive. The city remains the headquarters of the industry. The well-being of the metropolitan area is inseparably linked to the automotive industry.

The Depression generation naturally had its fears of future unemployment. These fears, however, have gradually been dissipated. Throughout much of the post-war interval, unemployment has been less than five percent of the total number of employables. Although the industrial employment of the early 1960's has tended to remain near or slightly below the 1958 level, there is a confidence in the future. The average hourly wage has risen each year since 1945. Higher weekly wages reflect not only the higher hourly rate, but also a considerable amount of overtime and other premium pay. The high per capita income of the metropolitan area should assure an enlargement of the service trades. The St. Lawrence Waterway should encourage the growth of foreign commerce.

Detroit has earnestly sought to reduce racial tensions. As early as 1945, Mayor Edward Jeffries appointed members to an inter-racial Committee. This group was the forerunner of many committees that enrolled members of both races in the cooperative task of building better relations. Education, housing, job opportunities, and other critical areas were boldly examined. In spite of many tensions, Detroit has been able to report progress in solving many issues and difficulties.

Detroit's task has been gigantic. During each decade, thousands of people have moved to Detroit to better their economic position. These newcomers have been cognizant of what they wanted in schools, transportation, and other municipal services. The major difficulties of rapid growth have been met. At the same time Detroit has continued its emphasis upon widespread opportunity.

Much, of course, remains to be done. Many of Detroit's pressures and problems lie below the surface. They are, perhaps, best sensed only by the long-term residents. The speed of social mobility gave rise to rapid change and old neighborhood structures disappeared with suddenness.

Fortunately, Detroit has been spared a public inertia. The entire metropolitan area has real assets in civic-minded individuals and organizations. In the metropolitan area are approximately 1,200 Protestant churches, 400 Roman Catholic churches and 50 synagogues. The area calls upon its churches and synagogues with frequency to aid in the development of a better civic life.

Industrial Detroit has the peculiar American ability to combine a touch of idealism with the highly practical.

APPENDIX A

Increase in Population in Detroit

1810 — 1,650
1820 — 1,442
1830 — 2,222
1840 — 9,124
1850 — 21,019
1860 — 45,619
1870 — 99,577
1880 — 116,340
1890 — 205,876
1900 — 285,704
1910 — 465,766
1920 — 993,675
1930 — 1,568,662
1940 — 1,623,452
1950 — 1,849,568
1960 — 1,670,144

APPENDIX B

Area of Detroit at Selected Dates

1806 — .33 sq. miles
1815 — 1.36 sq. miles
1850 — 5.85 sq. miles
1865 — 12 sq. miles
1900 — 23 sq. miles
1915 — 46 sq. miles
1921 — 79 sq. miles
1964 — 137 sq. miles

BIBLIOGRAPHY

Bald, Frederick. *Detroit's First American Decade,* 1796-1805. Ann Arbor, Michigan, 1948.

Bingay, Malcolm. *Detroit Is My Own Home Town.* New York, 1946.

Burton, Clarence. *The City of Detroit, Michigan.* 5 vols. Detroit, 1922.

Catlin, George. *The Story of Detroit.* Detroit, 1923.

Dain, Floyd. *Every House a Frontier.* Detroit, 1956.

Farmer, Silas. *The History of Detroit and Michigan.* 2 vols. Detroit, 1884.

Leake, Paul. *History of Detroit.* 3 vols. Chicago, 1912.

Miller, Raymond. *Kilowatts at Work.* Detroit, 1957.

Pare, George. *The Catholic Church in Detroit, 1701-1888.* Detroit, 1951.

Parkins, Alman. *The Historical Geography of Detroit.* Lansing, Michigan, 1918.

Pound, Arthur. *Detroit, Dynamic City.* New York, 1940.

Stark, George. *City of Destiny, The Story of Detroit.* Detroit, 1943.

Woodford, Frank. *Lewis Cass, the Last Jeffersonian.* New Brunswick, New Jersey, 1952.

——. *Mr. Jefferson's Disciple: a Life of Justice Woodward.* East Lansing, Michigan, 1953.

Woodford, Frank and Hyma, Albert. *Gabriel Richard.* Detroit, 1958.

Woodford, Frank and Mason, Philip. *Harper of Detroit.* Detroit, 1964.

INDEX

St. Anne's (Church), 11
St. Mary's Hospital, 45
Schoolcraft, Henry, 41
Scripps, James, 74
Shaarey Zedeck Jewish Society, 45
Shattuck, Lemuel, 41
Sheldon, John, 28, 42
Sisters of Charity, 45
Smith, John, 98
Stanley, J. M., 43

Temple Beth El, 65, 73
Theater, 44, 121
Toledo War, 34
Trevellick, Richard, 70
Trowbridge, Charles, 41

Underground Railroad, 47
University of Detroit, 119
University of Michigania, 27, 39

University of Michigan, 39
Upper Canada, 17

Van Antwerp, Eugene, 125

Walk-in-the-water, 26
War of 1812, 21, 22
Warren (Michigan), 113
Wayne, Anthony, 19
Wayne County, 125
Wayne County Farm, 46
Wayne State University, 118-19
Willcox, Orlando, 47
Williams, John, 33
Woodbridge, William, 35
Woodward, Augustus, 20, 27
Woodworth's Hotel, 25
World War I, 86-88
World War II, 114-16
Wronski, Thaddeus, 111
Wyandotte, 123